PAST IMPERFECT

Like earnest mastodons petrified in the forests of their own apparatus the archaeologists come and go. . . . Diligently working upon the refuse-heaps of some township for a number of years they erect on the basis of a few sherds or a piece of dramatic drainage, a sickly and enfeebled portrait of a way of life. How true it is, we cannot say; but if an Eskimo were asked to describe our way of life, deducing all his evidence from a search in a contemporary refuse dump, his picture might lack certain formidable essentials.

Lawrence Durrell, *Prospero's Cell*, (1962, p. 59)

There should be no need today, in 1971, to argue the case for the cultural work of the archaeologists . . . Additional finance is essential . . . enthusiastic volunteers are today carrying the great archaeological burden virtually unaided by the State.

There is no need to emphasise the growing interest in archaeology in this country.

For the most part the essential thing is to have time to record the details of any discovery before it is destroyed . . . once this work has been done, the destruction of the great majority of archaeological sites can be accepted as inevitable . . . We shall continue to watch the situation and will stand ready to consider the provision of further resources, if and when this should seem necessary. But whatever we can do in the Department of the Environment, we must continue to rely very greatly on the voluntary efforts of individual archaeologists and local societies whose services, and particularly whose vigilance, is essential and greatly valued.

Extracts from Parliamentary Debate, 16th December 1971. *Hansard* Vol. 326, No. 24, cols 1321–35

PAST IMPERFECT

The Story of Rescue Archaeology

Barri Jones

Heinemann · London

Heinemann Educational Books Ltd
22 Bedford Square, London WC1B 3HH

LONDON   EDINBURGH   MELBOURNE   AUCKLAND
HONG KONG   SINGAPORE   KUALA LUMPUR   NEW DELHI
IBADAN   NAIROBI   JOHANNESBURG
EXETER (NH)   KINGSTON   PORT OF SPAIN

ISBN 0 435 32974 X

Filmset in 'Monophoto' Baskerville
by Eta Services (Typesetters) Ltd, Beccles, Suffolk
Printed in Singapore by
Imago Publishing Ltd

Contents

List of Illustrations

List of Tables

Author's Note

The following organisations are referred to throughout the text:

Council for British Archaeology (CBA),
112 Kennington Road,
London SE11 6RE
01 582 0494

Directorate of Ancient Monuments and Historic Buildings
(referred to as 'Inspectorate')
Department of the Environment,
Fortress House,
23 Savile Row,
London W1X 2HE
01 734 6010

for Wales:
Central Office for Wales,
Gabalfa,
Cardiff CF4 4YF
0222 62131

for Scotland:
Argyll House,
Edinburgh EH3 7HF
031 225 5994/5

Rescue, A Trust for British Archaeology
15 Bull Plain,
Hertford,
Herts SG14 1DX
0992 58170

Author's Foreword and Acknowledgements

When this book was originally planned in 1976 I feared that it was impossible to predict, or find, a suitable ending to its story. That remained true in the writer's opinion until 1979–80 when finally some of the vital legislation designed to underpin the hard-won improvements in rescue archaeology passed on to the Statute Book. Change is still with us. Current government initiatives towards the privatisation of our historic heritage still make any absolute ending difficult to achieve, although most archaeologists would clearly recognise that the major period of far-reaching change that characterised much of the seventies is now at an end. To set that archaeological revolution – which has clearly shaped archaeology for the rest of the century in this country – in a true perspective, the final chapter has seen at least four major re-writings; not so some of the previous chapters where I have considered the story sufficiently complete without the addition of the very latest excavation results. This is particularly the case with London and York where the search to incorporate the results of current work would simply add successive codas to the story of an established pattern of work.

Yet, if the central core of these pages is the story of what was achieved, let us remember that during the 1970s important and specific opportunities for rescue excavation were lost not simply in York, London and some of the other major centres described in these pages but also at Bath, Bodmin, Carlisle, Colchester, Dundee, Edinburgh, Frome, Ipswich, Lancaster, Lewes, Nantwich, Perth, Radstock, Rochester, Salisbury, Shrewsbury, Tadcaster and above all New Palace Yard, Westminster (p. 57). Likewise, literally hundreds of miles of motorway (e.g. the M6 north of the Midlands, the M56, the M62 and the M80) and pipelines (notably the Frigg national gas pipelines from Scotland) were never subjected to any archaeological investigation.

It was to reverse this situation that Rescue, the Trust for British Archaeology was created in the early 1970s by a group of committed archaeologists. Often in conjunction with the Council for British Archaeology, it spearheaded many of the fundamental changes in British archaeology across the decade and was rarely afraid to criticise and campaign against inertia, red tape or vested interests in business or politics. As such this book is a legacy of both rescue archaeology at the time and the Rescue Trust in particular of which I had the honour to serve as Committee Member, Secretary and Trustee. Not surprisingly, therefore, as this book describes in part a corporate experience, my gratitude goes to those highly motivated archaeologists who saw that, if improvements were to be forthcoming, then the weapons of modern pressure groups rather than those of Academe had to be deployed, often, as it turned out, at the short-term expense of their career prospects.

Martin Biddle and Phil Barker were the first Chairman and Secretary of Rescue. Graham Thomas succeeded the former and benefited from the innovative skills of Robert Kiln, creator of the Rescue Awards, as Treasurer. As successful businessmen, they both retained a clear grasp of the longer term objectives and the importance of moulding the support of public opinion. Charles Thomas and Peter Fowler, at the time Chairman and Secretary of the Council for British Archaeology, later joined by Henry Cleere as Director, played a parallel role. Many of the moving figures amongst the archaeologists involved, such as Peter Addyman, Brian Hobley, Tom Hassall and Philip Mayes, ultimately became Unit Directors. Barry Cunliffe effectively promoted publicity for rescue archaeology nationally, as did Martin Walker, a new journalist on *The Guardian* in 1972 who astutely saw the nature of the revolution in archaeology, and made the subject very much his own along with Patricia Connor of *The Sunday Times*. Many of the insights or events described in this book go back to the individuals mentioned above and I am grateful to them as well as to Liz Thoms, Dorothy Lye, Kate Pretty, Clive Partridge and John Hunter for advice on specific points. The line drawings are the work of Dominic Powlesland. In its early draft the typescript benefited from the advice of Anthony Birley; latterly John Walker and Adrian Tindall, Sylvia Hazlehurst and Jasmin Vaccari helped bring the address list (pp. 153–8) up to date.

This is the first attempt to write a lengthy account of the rapid development of recent British archaeology. It is, of course, a subjective view that will not gain favour with everyone, particularly those who would prefer to think that change was inevitable and would have happened anyway through central agencies. To them I can only express the disagreement of one who tried to record the pressures from various sources that ultimately changed the face of practical archaeology in Britain.

Barri Jones
25 iv 83

Preface

Throughout much of Europe the mechanics of modern redevelopment are reshaping the visible and buried remains of the historic past. In Britain the process has been as swift as anywhere else, if not more so, as a result of the rapid growth of the motorway system and city-centre developments throughout the 1960s. The dominance of the car created both a plethora of multi-storey car parks that reshaped the centres of cities such as Gloucester, and the swathe of motorways that proved a double-edged tool in archaeologists' understanding of the density of rural settlement.

Perhaps it is the very richness of Britain's historic legacy that has created a spendthrift attitude towards the past. Even now 2,500 standing churches are potential candidates for redundancy and in some cases demolition. Yet, through the efforts of civic trusts and allied bodies, during the 1970s the campaign for adequate conservation of not simply the best but also the typical gained considerable ground. But the conservation movement has had only a limited effect on the below-ground problems of rescue archaeology. There are still conservationists who fail to realise that stratified archaeological deposits can represent just as important a contribution to the understanding of an historic centre as the surviving standing buildings. On most pre-twelfth-century sites in many of Britain's historic towns, the archaeological deposits often form the only documentation available. Yet in the early 1970s in only 17 of 457 historic centres was any adequate standard of archaeological investigation under way.

This was a stark fact that became evident from *The Erosion of History*, a survey produced for the Council for British Archaeology (CBA) in 1972 and designed to bring the problem home to planners, archaeologists and public alike. It was a fundamental document that in many ways heralded the era of rescue archaeology. Though its legislative recommendations long awaited any kind of recognition, the survey had a seminal effect in altering the attitude of planners towards archaeology and in focusing the aims of archaeologists away from the glamorous and easy, towards the technically difficult problems of urban rescue work that can often provide the only documentation for the early history of a town. At the same time the growing mass of published material following finds during motorway construction in the 1960s and 1970s brought about a fundamental change in understanding the later prehistoric, Romano-British and medieval countryside. Such work, backed up on occasion by co-ordinated programmes of aerial survey, brought about a quantitative revolution in rural archaeology by showing that ancient occupation was on a far more densely populated scale than had previously been realised.

These developments in archaeology in the 1970s are described in the present book. They go far beyond the realms of pure archaeology into the world of property developers, government finance and legislation, as well as local authority politics. This book cannot attempt to recount every development, but selects the significant in the progress of rescue archaeology during that decade. Because of the close relationship with the modern battlefield of 'planning', a straightforward account of important excavations, without any indication of how the various projects were established, would be difficult to justify today. *Past Imperfect* has inevitably been written with the knowledge that success in the field of rescue excavation relates directly to individuals, and to their ability and determination to ensure the presence of archaeological awareness in the modern spectrum of planning and development. The battles of rescue archaeology were fought, won or lost by individuals who firmly believed in what they were undertaking. And this book is dedicated to those individuals who helped to shape archaeology as it is today.

G. D. B. J. 1982

The author and publishers would like to thank the following for permission to reproduce photographs and other material in this book (numbers in brackets give the pages on which the material appears):

Robert H. Bewley (115); Department of Archaeology, University of Southampton (73); Guildhall Library, City of London (124); Her Majesty's Stationery Office (66, 67); Museum of London (129, 131); C. R. Musson, Rescue Archaeology Group (98); Perth High Street Archaeological Excavation (119); Rescue (The British Archaeological Group) (55, 66, 67, 71, 73, 74, 94).

I
Introduction

By the mid-1970s an average of half a million people every year visited the remains of Hadrian's Wall; press and television coverage of any important archaeological discovery (and some not so important!) was accepted by the public as a matter of course. In the context of such general interest, debates in the House of Lords, newspaper leaders and television films served to deepen awareness of the underlying issues of archaeology. Meanwhile in the archaeological field itself, central government spending on rescue excavation leapt from under a quarter of a million pounds in 1970 to over two millions within six years. Local authority expenditure in funding official archaeologists, excavation and publication probably ran at a comparable figure. Likewise there was a revolution in archaeological methods particularly in the recording of complicated and deeply stratified excavations. There was a rapid advance in both method and approach, in logistics, in strategy, in techniques, and in public information, amongst archaeologists as a whole. During the 1970s archaeology entered into a dynamic stage of development. It was one of the two areas of fastest university expansion and became the area of greatest public interest in extra-mural teaching.

How did this new situation arise? How did it affect the thinking of public and archaeologist alike? Underlying these questions is the fundamental one of why the public should be interested in archaeology at all. The answer is perhaps tripartite: psychological, if one accepts that the purpose of archaeology lies in the recreation (whether literal or otherwise) of the past for generations present and to come; practical, in that, unlike geology and some of the other classic disciplines where his role has all but disappeared, the amateur still has a significant part to play in archaeology; and environmental, because that is the area in which rescue archaeology predominantly makes demands on the public conscience.

Public and local authorities had to assess what value society was prepared to place on its archaeological past and what financial and material provision it was prepared to make for the investigation, recording and occasional preservation of that heritage. This attitude, encouraged by the dominance of rescue archaeology, was responsible for a radical change in public opinion. Rescue archaeology, as it is termed, is archaeological research undertaken to survey or excavate monuments, sites, groups of sites, even extensive surviving ancient landscapes threatened with serious alteration or destruction. Some professional purists have clung to the idea fashionable in the university circles of the 1950s, that rescue archaeology is necessarily hasty and therefore inferior. Although this attitude still lingers on in Britain, by the mid-1970s, practically every major, and the great majority of minor, excavations belonged to the rescue category. By then they were largely the result of careful forward planning and arguably outstripped (thanks to the greater finance involved) the results of most self-styled 'pure research' projects.

The reason for the success of many rescue projects is simple. In reality, at their best there is no difference between rescue and research work. If a rescue project is to represent a valid and acceptable expenditure of public funds (most work in this category receives a subvention of 50 per cent or more from government sources), then it must be seen as a carefully planned and well-organised operation. This became essential in order to avoid the possibility of adverse public, and therefore local authority, reaction, but also because the actual rescue excavation in many cases represents only a fraction of what might have been done. Many newly-discovered sites rarely received any adequate attention during the brief period between discovery and development. Many known ones went by the board because within archaeologically rich areas local or regional academic priorities had to be observed. Such priorities affect the logistics of any proper operation: the various functions—survey and recording, excavation, conservation, back-ground research and full publication—demand such a compression of effort in both time and finance that only selective rescue work could be carried out in the richer archaeological sites and zones.

With the spectrum of rescue threats—city-centre redevelopments, ring road and motorway building, quarrying, deep ploughing—that caused the loss of more of Britain's archaeological heritage during the 1970s than ever before, the archaeologists were ill-armed to face their task. Their organisational structure was increasingly unsuited to their aspirations, depending as it did on local, regional or national bodies that in many areas were purely traditional or, at worst, random solutions to modern problems. With the significantly increased funds available it became essential that a structure for rescue work be created to utilise what resources there were in the most effective manner. The problem had both internal and external facets. Professional archaeology had to put its own house in order and, at the same time, try to eliminate any featherbedding of specially favoured projects or regions by cutting the financial cake more equitably. Archaeologists engaged in rescue work

Fig. 1 A mechanical excavator destroys the 12-foot standing remains of the Roman legionary bath-house, Chester 1968

had to organise themselves logically and account for rescue funds received in a way that the public could readily appreciate; they were anxious to present their work in a manner that the public could recognise as part of a planned research programme with historical questions and answers.

Public involvement was the external facet of the problem. There are rescue excavations that take place in remote rural areas but these are a tiny minority: the majority take place in the centres of Britain's historic towns and cities. In such situations archaeology cannot be considered in isolation, as a self-justified academic activity: it is but one of the many clamouring aspects of the environmental question, its proponents appearing to the public and to local government as yet another pressure group within the influential environmentalist movement.

In the urban context rescue archaeology has had to sell itself to create the situations and gain the financial support that it requires for survival. Despite a few shining successes there were many failures, and indeed many would say that rescue archaeology is losing the battle in the major civic centres. Nonetheless, thanks to public support, by the late 1970s rescue archaeology had reached a new level of acceptance, indicated by the incorporation of archaeologists into many local authority structures.

2
The Growth of Modern Archaeology

In the early decades of the twentieth century the professional archaeologists of Britain were few in number. There were some posts in the departments of the British Museum, paralleled by other keepers in the national museums of Wales and Scotland and the university museums of Oxford and Cambridge. But provincial museums functioned largely through the enthusiasm of part-time volunteers and were linked administratively to the newly constituted public library services, introduced in 1907 (and whose imminent demise was confidently predicted). There also existed two or three university chairs (their holders normally combining the role of ancient historian with archaeologist), isolated from both supporting staff and laboratory facilities. As well as these, the nascent Royal Commissions and the Ancient Monuments Inspectorate of His Majesty's Office of Works supported a small number of posts on derisory salaries. In addition O. G. S. Crawford, pioneer archaeologist/geographer, had in a sense personally created the post of archaeological officer within a somewhat reluctant Ordnance Survey as a prelude to the production of the period maps for which that organisation was rightly famous; and abroad there were the directors of the two principal British Schools, in Rome and in Athens. Thus, including the secretaries of a few learned societies, the title of professional archaeologist could not properly be extended beyond more than 30 or 40 persons in this country at that time.

This paucity of personnel did not, of course, imply lack of progress or competence in archaeology. But it did mean that the number of excavations was small and that much of the work was executed by people who earned their daily bread elsewhere: teachers, doctors, clerics and the squirearchy, and perhaps above all, ancient historians such as R. G. Collingwood who did much valuable work. Then things began to change. By the 1930s the Office of Works and the Royal Commissions had created more and better paid posts in the Civil Service. A handful of universities were offering archaeological courses, sometimes with scientific research facilities to back them up. At the same time the Museums Association, treading the same path as the Library Association, formed

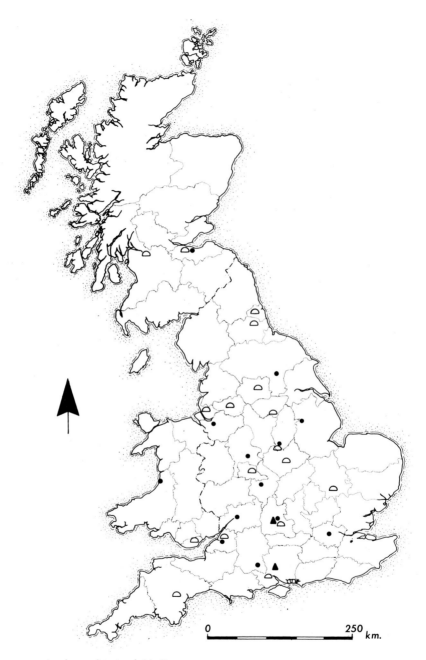

▲ *Archaeological Units*

◠ *Universities with Archaeology Departments*

• *Field Officers*

Fig. 2   Diagram showing the distribution of field archaeologists in 1970

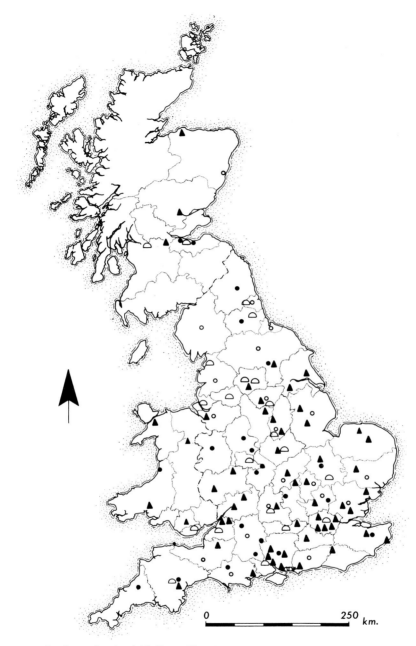

- ▲ *Archaeological Units or Trusts*
- ◠ *Universities with Archaeology Departments*
- ● *Field Officers*
- ○ *County Archaeologists*

Fig. 3   Diagram showing the distribution of field archaeologists in 1976

a professional body which in itself helped expand the number of permanent posts available.

The Second World War brought further major changes, if rather slow, in its aftermath. The creation of new universities and the expansion of existing ones, particularly those in the provinces, built up a far greater range of academic posts, often with adequate support facilities. The opportunity for training in practical excavation on bomb-damaged sites, especially in London under Professor Grimes, fed the upsurge of both undergraduate and public interest in the material remains of Britain's past. The popularity of the programme 'Animal, Vegetable or Mineral?' (two of the protagonists, Glyn Daniel and Sir Mortimer Wheeler, were voted TV Personalities of the Year) was evidence of this growing public interest which coincided with the great expansion in higher education and an increasing number of students anxious to read archaeology courses; imaginations were also fired by a new kind of historical fiction written for both children and adults, from the pens of such writers as Rosemary Sutcliffe, Mary Stuart and Mary Renault.

By the 1960s archaeology had finally broken away from the status of geology which it had had in the 1890s—the part-time preoccupation of a few specialists and amateurs. For the first time the general public began to feel involved in archaeological issues, and, whereas this involvement had previously been encouraged only by isolated pioneers, such as Sir Mortimer Wheeler in the 1920s, and had occasionally caused considerable professional antagonism, now it was recognised by the bulk of professional archaeologists. As more and more people realised that urban renewal, motorway development and the long-term effects of deep-ploughing offered fresh archaeological opportunities, and that the unglamorous task of archaeologically dismembering town centres offered at least as much potential information as operations on sun-soaked hill-forts, archaeology began to take its place in the environmental fields.

It is worth emphasising that the archaeological profession has never been united by a common vocational training such as is provided, for example, for doctors and dentists. Archaeologists are spawned from a plethora of sources: from the 1960s, scientists, particularly those involved with the earth sciences, joined those who were trained on more conventional arts courses at universities in the 1950s and 1960s. The trend towards a more uniform professionalism by the early 1970s, stemmed from the greatly increasing number of archaeologists in the country. A comparison between Fig. 2 and Fig. 3 shows the great growth of the subject in terms of personnel that took place over six years from 1970. Expanding university departments and museum staff accounted for much of the growth, but the Ancient Monuments

Inspectorate of the Department of the Environment and the Royal Commissions were also expanding their professional staff. The newcomers to the profession were beginning to be drawn increasingly from the relatively new archaeology departments in universities and this meant that more and more archaeologists were coming to share a common student training background (although no university course would claim to be strictly vocational in purpose, and, indeed, many students take an archaeology course from a desire to study a different kind of social history).

If there has been a growing uniformity of general background one important distinction continues to separate archaeologists from many other professions. Their career patterns have fallen among a very dispersed range of professions. Archaeologists have found themselves as university academics, civil servants, museum staff, or, increasingly, in local government at county, or even district level: a most important development of the 1970s was the growth of county archaeologists, or their equivalents, placed within the planning departments of various organisations. The late emergence of the subject accounts in part for this spread of professions, but the main reason is that a wide variety of skills and training enables people to call themselves archaeologists and to be employed as such. Indeed, the variety of skills required means that they can rarely all be combined in one person. Mastery of all the techniques required for modern excavation is not an essential prerequisite for a professional archaeologist, and would, in fact, be a near impossibility. Moreover, the pressures of work in local government perhaps rightly debar many from much practical work. Others have no taste for digging, while there are those who concentrate on the scientific analysis of the products of excavation, particularly of evidence relating to the ancient environment. Attempts to form a professional body to promote recognised standards of competence were long thwarted across the seventies but finally came to fruition in 1982.

At the same time the understanding of archive material became better channelled in the 1970s. There also came into being in Britain a growing band of excavators without formal professional qualifications but with a broad background of experience. Many began by applying their interest at school and later as volunteers at excavations organised by the Department of the Environment. They form a considerable force deployed in British archaeology, partly involved in seasonal work and partly occupying posts as journeymen excavators in rescue archaeology units. Their approach is, of course, novel: they see the actual practice of excavation as the essence of archaeology, and rightly seek professional recognition for their skill and experience in the field.

The steady growth in the number of archaeologists could not have taken place without an increasing awareness both at the professional,

9

and, later at the public level, of the need to record and, where appropriate, conserve the remains of a heritage under the threat of destruction or redevelopment. Yet the development of a concept of rescue archaeology is not an easy one to trace. Perhaps it began with William Morris. He observed repair work on Tewkesbury Abbey in the late nineteenth century and was appalled by the cavalier fashion in which the remains of the medieval buildings were being destroyed or modified beyond recognition and without record.

This concern was for a standing building and it took a considerable time before public interest extended below ground: archaeology was primarily field archaeology, the archaeology of upstanding monuments in the countryside. The next step in a growing awareness appears to have been the creation of Royal Commissions on Ancient and Historical Monuments in England, Scotland and Wales in the first decade of this century. However, the role of the Commissions lay not in excavations but in the meticulous recording of field remains on a county basis: the idea of rescue excavation was still not formalised.

One of the earliest premeditated excavations occurred at Flint in North Wales in 1924. A series of discoveries relating to the Roman lead industry on Deeside made it clear that a certain area had a considerable archaeological potential. Since the area concerned, the Ship Field, was, in the excavator's view, 'ripe for building ... it was decided to concentrate on it in an endeavour to obtain, so far as possible, in the limited time available, more detailed knowledge of this portion of the Roman site of Flint' (*Flintshire Historical Journal*, 1924). Sure enough, the area was built over within 18 months, but much useful information was gained from the prior excavations. Similar motivation governed the excavation of a Roman villa site between Bristol and Keynsham at about the same time.

The 1920s were archaeologically exciting, and leading the field were such outstanding figures as O. G. S. Crawford, Cyril Fox and Mortimer Wheeler. The new tool of aerial photography, so dramatically propagandised by Crawford throughout the decade, allowed a vastly greater understanding of the buried landscape. Hundreds more sites became known, in many cases yielding to the aerial camera much of their layout without the use of the spade. Accompanying the developments was much animated discussion; the pages of Crawford's new journal, *Antiquity*, rang with it, and, from the evidence of his autobiography, R. G. Collingwood, was an eager participant.

Most of the arguments that were used in the early years of the modern rescue movement first appeared in the 1920s. In 1928, at the height of the summer drought, a Royal Air Force photographer flying over the site of Caistor-by-Norwich, capital of the Iceni of Norfolk, and an important city of Roman Britain, had taken a photograph which showed the street grid and much of the internal layout. Amid much excitement an excavation committee was formed but Mortimer Wheeler raised the question of the 'need' for such work.

> How far is the excavation of Caistor a justifiable outlay of energy and money at the present time? The Britisher, is, by nature, opportunist, and in his involved and muddled way, generally at prodigious cost, he has the habit of winning through in the end. For that very reason he is inclined to raise muddle to the rank of a fetish and regard it as a national virtue. But even a virtue, overwritten, is liable to tire. Romano-British archaeology is a case in point. During the past ten years we have been hacking up this Roman Britain of ours, with unprecedented zest. Some of the work has been fruitless through mere incompetence; some has been equally fruitless through the lack of adequate publication; some has been fruitful, and we can honestly say that our knowledge of Roman Britain has in certain directions increased generously during the period. But how much effort has been wasted both in detail and in bulk, from the absence of a concerted plan of campaign! A certain element of opportunism is inevitable, a threatened site, even of secondary importance, must be excavated or at least trenched before it is permanently lost . . . Apart, however, from instances such as this the time is ripe for some central and influential body to bring order into chaos.
>
> *Antiquity* III, 10 (1929, p. 186)

Wheeler's questioning of the underlying motives reflects an important development in thinking at the time.

> Economically the excavation of Caistor at the present time can be justified only insofar as it enlists those purely local interests to which the wider issues are not likely to appeal. For those who are able to take a more comprehensive view of the present and pressing requirements of Romano-British archaeology, it must be clear that, at the moment when our only available legionary fortress [Caerleon], our premier Roman colony [Colchester] and our only Roman municipality [Verulamium] are all in an actual or potential danger of obliteration, the excavation of this remote Norfolk cornfield is a luxury that could well have been deferred.
>
> (ibid., p. 187)

Roman archaeology tended to dominate thinking at the time, certainly to the detriment of the development of techniques of large-scale open area excavations of the kind that were already being attempted in other parts of Northern Europe. In a remarkable passage written in the same year, Crawford anticipated practically every argument concerning organisation and objectives that were to be used in the 1970s, even the idea of land purchase to conserve archaeological sites as part of an archaeological and cultural heritage.

> It is too often assumed nowadays that excavation if properly conducted is always and everywhere a good thing. That is not so. There are only two excuses for undertaking an excavation: the acquisition of valuable know-

ledge, or the imminent destruction of a site. If a site is to be covered by buildings evidence will be destroyed and excavation at some remote date will be made more difficult. If a site is being destroyed for ever by the removal of soil in bulk, obviously there will be nothing left to dig. Under such circumstances imperfect examination and a defective record are better than none . . .

Here we come up against the besetting sin of provincialism. So far as our national interest is organised at all it is organised by counties, and what might be a powerful body of opinion is robbed of most of its force by being split up into forty-eight or more parts. Consequently, we have the absurd spectacle of two groups in two neighbouring counties, the one trying unsuccessfully to collect the miserable sum required to excavate a threatened site before it is too late, the other raising a substantial sum to carry out a wholly unnecessary dig on a site of no urgent importance . . .

Conservation, not excavation, is the need of the day; conservation, not only of purely archaeological features, but of the amenities which give them more than half their charm. Who cares for Oldbury and St George's Hill now that they are infested with villas? What is the use of preserving the walls of a village if the site of the village they protected is to be built over? . . .

In most instances, nothing short of the purchase of land is of the slightest use, though in others an intelligent application of the Town Planning Act may suffice. The need is really urgent; for with the approaching electrification of Southern England, the coniferous activities of the Woods and Forests Department and of private planters, the demands of the Services, for land, for aeroplanes and manoeuvres, the spread of bungaloid eruptions and the threat of arterial roads and ribbon development—with all these terrors imminent it is unlikely that any open country or downland will be left in southern England in a hundred years time. Salisbury Plain is already ruined; Sussex Downs are threatened. Dorset and Dartmoor, however, survive, and the Cotswolds though less prolific in pre-historic sites are still entirely agricultural and unspoilt. A far-sighted policy would gradually acquire large portions and keep them for posterity . . .

Antiquity III, 9 (1929, p. 1 ff.)

There were other voices in the debate. R. G. Collingwood, through his father, W. G. Collingwood, had been reared on the northern archaeology of Hadrian's Wall, where, thanks to the stereotype plans of Roman forts and camps, it was often possible to answer historical problems by excavating relatively small trenches. This approach influenced Collingwood deeply and he was worried by the prevailing tendencies elsewhere. He had clearly set his face against random excavation or what he termed 'blind digging', whether in a rescue context or otherwise.

In the south, when I began to frequent the rooms of the Society of Antiquaries, I found a very different state of things. Excavation was still being done according to the principles laid down by General Pitt-Rivers in the last quarter of the nineteenth century. Pitt-Rivers was a very great archaeologist and a supreme master in the technique of excavation; but ... [he] dug in order to see what he could find out. He had not applied to archaeology the famous advice of Lord Acton, 'study problems not periods' ... The idea of excavation was to choose a site: to uncover it systematically, one piece each year, pouring thousands of pounds into the work, till it was all dug; and then go on to another. The result was that, although museums were choked with the finds, amazingly little (as it now appears) was discovered about the history of the site.

From *An Autobiography* by R. G. Collingwood (1939, pp. 83–4)
Reprinted by permission of Oxford University Press

From his particular ivory tower Collingwood took a somewhat dismissive view of the public.

The public (including persons of all grades of wealth, from rich bankers and industrialists downward) cared little or nothing for historical knowledge. If you want a lever to extract money from a public for an excavation you must not tell them that it will yield the solution for important historical problems. Natural scientists can say that kind of thing ... but archaeologists have to use as their lever that nostalgic self-loathing which is so characteristic of our times. 'Here is a romantic ancient site', they must say, 'which is about to be covered with revolting bungalows, hideous bypass roads, and so forth. Give us your guineas, so that we can find whatever is to be found there before our chance is gone for ever.' Thus instead of being chosen for excavation because it contains the solution of a burning problem, a site is excavated for non-scientific reasons, exactly as in the old days.

(ibid.)

Collingwood's approach was reactivated in the backlash against rescue archaeology in the late 1970s and is the background to the 'research versus rubbish collection' argument. Most modern archaeologists would argue that Collingwood made insufficient distinction between salvage excavation and the longer-term rescue work that has considerable research potential built into it. Long-term rescue projects such as the excavation of the Upper Brook Street site at Winchester, begun in 1961, rank among the forefront of work with major research results in Britain.

Collingwood also mentions the large number of excavations being conducted and the pressure this created in storing finds and publishing reports before the next excavations. The accelerated rate of excavation was to a considerable extent due to the growth in the 1930s of an archaeological section within the Office of Works under the direction of J. P. Bushe-Fox. Bushe-Fox was himself a remarkable excavator, but clearly the academics were worried by the increasing trail of unpublished excavation reports left by members of the growing bureaucracy. According to Collingwood,

Every man who is engaged in scientific work of any kind knows that it is a fundamental obligation of scientific morality to publish your results. When the work is archaeological excavation the duty is a peculiarly urgent one, because the site once thoroughly excavated is a site from which no future archaeologist would ever be able to find out anything . . . all archaeologists know this, all except the official archaeologists of the British government act accordingly. British government archaeologists are constantly excavating sites all over the country, at the taxpayers' expense, without publishing any reports at all. They know that they are committing the fundamental crime against their own science; because when other archaeologists speak to them about it they have their excuse ready. The Treasury will not allow the money for publication.

(ibid.)

The complaint is one that has since been central to archaeology. Yet Collingwood's argument shows significantly the development of social attitudes by the 1930s. While Crawford had pleaded eloquently for intervention to purchase archaeological sites for conservation or excavation, Collingwood talked of British government archaeologists and saw the issue lying much more firmly in the hands of a part of central government. By 1939 he, along with others, saw the need for a state archaeological service that would be established on a broad basis and concerned not simply with excavation, but also with the protection and conservation of sites of archaeological importance.

We may hope perhaps that scholars will in time compel all the government officials responsible for looking after our ancient monuments to treat them not as objects of sentimental pilgrimage but as potential sources of historical knowledge.

(ibid.)

These aspirations were, of course, checked by the outbreak of the Second World War.

The post-War years saw the gradual development of government archaeology from its early days. The development became rapid during the 1970s although it did not reach the comprehensive provision of a state archaeology service as found in several other European countries. In 1969 the Inspectorate of Ancient Monuments became part of the newly-formed Department of the Environment under the wing of the Secretary of State for Urban Affairs. Having developed historically from the pre-War Office of Works, via a branch of the Ministry of Public Building and Works, it has many of the disadvantages of a small unit within a mammoth bureaucratic structure. Sections within the Inspectorate deal with the upkeep of standing monuments in guardianship, scheduling, rescue excavation and publication. The teeth of the operation lie with the main inspectors. The post of Chief Inspector is supported by a Principal Inspector who is primarily responsible for the co-ordination of finance and the organisation of regional inspectors. These inspectors are responsible for administrative regions, often of daunting size. Inspectors in Wales and Scotland operate under roughly similar arrangements, part-academics, still expecting to conduct their own excavations, part bureaucrats responsible for channelling the needs of scheduling and excavation in their areas. In this task they had, for a brief period in the late 1970s, the help of an academic advisory committee for each area, and at national level an Ancient Monuments Board further advises the Chief Inspector, notably through a sub-committee concerned solely with rescue archaeology. In the early 1980s, however, fundamental change was being introduced following a Parliamentary Bill which will remove many of the Inspectorate's functions.

In the 1970s, however, the Inspectorate initiated substantial change in the organisation of archaeology in Britain. Most important was the financial improvement triggered, at least initially, by the public pressure of the rescue archaeology movement. In the 1950s and 1960s there was no such public involvement and the role and financial power of the Inspectorate remained relatively static. If major change was to come, then it might have sprung from two other areas. Crawford and, more precisely, Collingwood, had looked to an increasing involvement of central government in archaeology. They had not considered the possible involvement of local authorities, which, normally at county level, was to grow effectively in the 1970s; nor had they dreamt that one excavation programme could change the face of British archaeology through individual initiative.

The importance of the Winchester research unit for the archaeology of the 1960s was that it constituted a prototype for many of the similar developments that grew up during the late 1960s and early 1970s. In the early 1960s archaeology in the field was still dominated by the universities, more especially since excavation was normally conceived of as a discontinuous process conducted in the summer interval between academic terms and rarely in an urban rescue context. When, at the end of the 1950s the potential of larger-scale excavation was realised at Winchester, the initial excavations were still conducted as the academic forays typical of the time. However, in 1961 Martin Biddle took the remarkable step of resigning his lectureship at Exeter University in favour of the insecure role of establishing and maintaining the permanent excavation project at Winchester. As director of the first major urban archaeology unit in Britain, he was to gain professional status and influence.

Fundamental to Biddle's decision was a swing of emphasis away from a concept of excavation dominated by the requirements of a particular

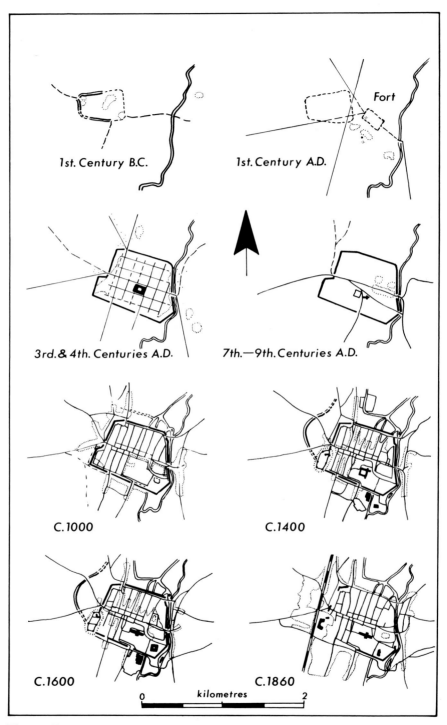

Fig. 4 Diagram showing the development of Winchester from the first century BC to the nineteenth century

period, notably that of Roman Britain, towards the examination without period bias of a city or town as an overall archaeological entity. This approach was strongly advocated by Biddle in a series of articles, and ultimately led to the creation of the Council for British Archaeology's Urban Research Committee in 1968, and to its publication in 1972, of *The Erosion of History*. This was the first overall assessment of the archaeological potential of the towns of Britain that may be seen as marking a turning point in the growth of rescue archaeology.

Why was Winchester so important? Academically it was a logical choice in being a city where Roman and, in particular, post-Roman history could be demonstrated beyond doubt. Capital of the kingdom of Wessex, and long one of the most important cities of southern Britain, it was arguably a product of the new town planning of the later Saxon period. The core of the modern city had shrunk within the perimeter of the original city walls, leaving areas of early and late medieval occupation relatively intact. Lower Brook Street, in the north-eastern angle of the town, was a case in point. There, in an area that was due for redevelopment, long-term rescue excavation produced a major research achievement in showing the development and social history of the quarter from the Iron Age to the late medieval period. For instance, above the Roman levels timber and stone buildings of the eighth and ninth centuries gave way to the small church of St Mary, which was, from the twelfth to thirteenth century set amongst rows of cottages for artisan workers in the cloth-finishing industry.

This work on a dwelling area was linked with specific excavations of the Anglo-Saxon Old Minster, immediately north of the cathedral, and the Anglo-Saxon palace nearby. The former produced evidence for the tomb of St Swithin at its west end, and the Anglo-Saxon palace excavation was followed by examination of the Norman Wolvesey Palace of the succeeding period. All in all, the work of the Winchester research unit produced the first detailed picture of the growth of an historic city. Moreover, the methods of excavation involving the intricacies of working on timber buildings set the standard for the following decade of urban archaeology.

The lessons of Winchester were rapidly applied in nearby Southampton. The city of Southampton had been extensively bombed in the Second World War and, as a result, prior to redevelopment, many of the sites to be excavated lay derelict. Southampton Water has always been a major trade artery, and in the Saxon period much of Winchester's trade doubtless passed along it. Remarkably, however, the central settlement changed its site from period to period. In Roman Britain the town of Clausentum had developed in a bend in the river at Bitterne; in the Saxon period, a beach market had developed across the

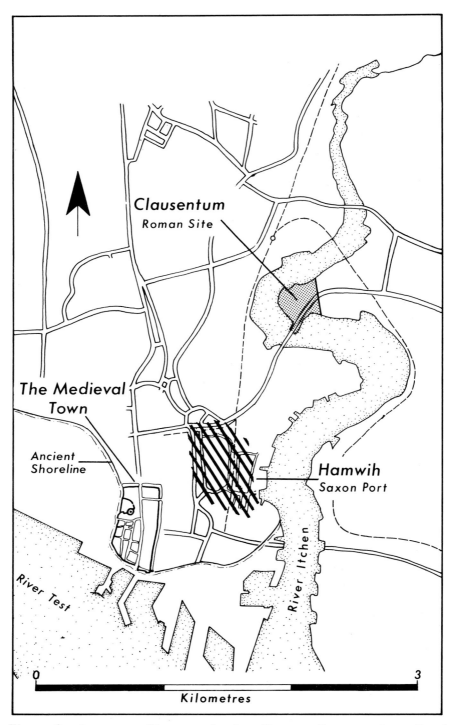

Fig. 5 Southampton. Diagram showing Roman, Saxon and medieval developments

river at Hamwih. Despite the difficulties of excavations from the 1960s for Peter Addyman and other archaeologists from Southampton University, and later the urban excavation unit, the finds alone were sufficient to demonstrate that extensive cultural and economic links had existed with the Continent. These links were maintained when the actual population centre moved further west to become the medieval town of Southampton located around the present dock area.

One of the other early effective rescue excavation programmes was established at Oxford. The city was undergoing a major redevelopment cycle from the late 1960s, not in the area of the ancient colleges but to the west where the surviving castle mound still serves as a visible reminder of the medieval nucleus flanking a tributary of the Thames. Iron Age and Romano-British farms are known to have existed in the city area, but Oxford's history as a city rather than as a cluster of farmsteads really began in the Saxon period when, in AD 727, according to tradition St Frideswide established a religious house on or near the site of the present cathedral. Around the gates of this monastery and strung out along the roads leading into modern Oxford a small lay settlement sprang into life. It was this settlement, excavated by Tom Hassall, director of the nascent Oxford Archaeological Unit, and his team in the late 1960s, that became a flourishing centre and one of the chief meeting places of the royal council in the late Saxon period. The addition of a Norman castle on the west side of the site in AD 1071 marked the next stage in the development of the medieval centre from which the university town developed.

Just as Peter Addyman's excavation team had shown at Hamwih, so the new unit established at Oxford revealed that it was in the historically blank Saxon period that the new art of urban rescue excavation could make its greatest contribution. But in view of the complex stratified deposits, and the nature of the timber buildings involved, for example, at Winchester and Oxford, it was clear that new standards of excavation, recording and archaeological interpretation were required. Ultimately, too, it was equally clear that new forms of archaeological publication would need to be forthcoming to cope with the vast mass of material recovered from urban sites.

At the same time, as new and higher standards of excavation were being set amongst the extremely complex stratigraphy of urban rescue sites, Phil Barker of Birmingham University was making a somewhat different contribution. On the very late levels in the centre of the Romano-British city of Wroxeter he was showing that extremely meticulous excavation at the bottom of the plough soil could produce the minimal evidence for fifth- and sixth-century buildings, either built in timber or almost completely destroyed by subsequent agriculture. His work was based on large-scale, open area excavations, and in one sense marked a reaffirmation of the principles established by Scandinavian archaeologists who had demonstrated that only by the clearance of very substantial areas and the comparison of soil coloration and other minutiae could the plans of such post-Roman buildings be devined. The message of Barker's work at Wroxeter and his diligent analysis of the early medieval castle at Hen Domen in the Welsh Marches reinforced the movement towards higher standards of recording and of interpretation of excavations.

The formation in the early days of rescue archaeology, of excavation units at Winchester, Southampton and Oxford, had widespread ramifications. Wherever redevelopment schemes were afoot archaeologists were immediately brought into the world of the planner: the long-term assimilation of rescue archaeology into local authority planning was just beginning. Meanwhile, the sheer pace of redevelopment in various historic centres such as Lincoln, Colchester and Chester forced the creation of other *de facto* excavation units, by the pressure of archaeological and public opinion. Many of these nascent organisations were independent. They drew their financial support from the Department of Environment, from what grants they could raise from local authorities and, in some cases from the actual site developers. They were helped by much voluntary labour, both in the trenches and at post-excavation stage. The growth of excavation units can really be seen as a response to the pressures of urban redevelopment. Most of the historic town centres of Britain have undergone development projects that have threatened to destroy a great deal of material evidence of the town's past: in general there are very few documents that relate to the history of the British town prior to the twelfth century, and greater knowledge can only derive from archaeological evidence.

The fate of the various historic cities was long a matter of concern for the Council for British Archaeology through its Urban Research Committee, and, after 1971, the newly-established Trust for British Archaeology. *The Erosion of History*, sought to quantify the scale of the problem with alarming conclusions. The layout of new roads, particularly in a relief system, and overall building developments, whether planned or piecemeal, often destroys not only the evidence of a detailed topography of the more historic centres, but also the archaeological deposits that in many cases, such as at York, Gloucester, Lincoln and London, form almost the only surviving evidence for the detailed history of the town's development prior to the twelfth century.

It can be said that, since the Second World War, the historic city centres of Britain have undergone cycles of redevelopment. In cities like Sheffield such a cycle can be regarded as having been completed in the years immediately following the War, while in other centres, such as

York and Lincoln, the massive process of modern redevelopment really began its upward swing in the late 1960s.

Gloucester is a major centre where the cycle of central redevelopment has declined (Fig. 28). In little over 10 years, between 1960 and 1971, 10 acres or roughly a quarter of the area once enclosed by the Roman walls—the heart of the historic city—were rebuilt. In over three of the 10 acres involved in the redevelopment area, basements were constructed causing the archaeological levels beneath the ground to be wholly removed. Over the remaining seven acres the beds of concrete piles on which new buildings are invariably placed, together with the excavation for pile caps, service ducts, water tanks, lift shafts, and so on, all irreparably damaged the archaeological evidence. Unfortunately, the scale and pace of destruction of the evidence of the past is not unique to Gloucester. Just such disaster befell the major Roman building opposite the Temple of Claudius at Colchester, destroyed without examination during the construction of a supermarket in the early 1970s.

Destruction of a city beneath ground level has been more than matched by the rate of demolition of historic buildings above it. For example, in the 20 years following the Ministry of Housing's 1950 list, over 60 per cent of Gloucester's listed timber-framed buildings were demolished. All the same, there was an archaeological response. The appointment of Henry Hurst as a full-time City Archaeological Officer, initially for a period of four years from 1968, was subsequently extended in view of the pressures during the 1970s, and he and his successor, Carolyn Heighway, did a great deal to salvage the history of Roman and medieval Gloucester.

The redevelopment of Lincoln was later than that of Gloucester. Lincoln is one of the most archaeologically important towns in the country. It contains the remains of a Roman legionary fortress that was transformed into a colony, which extended it downhill towards the River Witham and the heart of the modern city (see Fig. 26, p. 81). In the medieval period a castle and a cathedral dominated the skyline overlooking the city in much the same way as they still do today. During the 1970s there was much controversy over Lincoln at both archaeological and political levels. The two are intertwined because decisions of a political nature have ultimately controlled the location and speed of redevelopment programmes. This is demonstrated in Lincoln's case which illustrates clearly what is meant by the redevelopment of a large area of a historic city centre.

Development plans were first prepared in 1972 (see Table 1). Delays in the progress of the work meant that parts of the programme were still awaiting construction at the *end of the decade*. In terms of area Lincoln presents in some ways greater archaeological problems than Gloucester or Colchester: at Lincoln the Roman colony that formed the basis of all

TABLE 1   Lincoln: redevelopment proposals in the early 1970s

Outline Date	Site	Description
Early 1972	St Paul in the Bail (Phase 1)	Preliminary work on potential Saxon and medieval churches. Possibly the earliest church in Lincoln, according to Bede, dedicated in AD 625. Known site of legional *principia* and its successor (forum?). Key site in the upper colonia: work anticipated over several seasons.
Summer 1972	Flaxengate	Major redevelopment? For government offices? The site was one of the largest blocks available for excavation in the lower colonia. Little known of the lower colonia layout but in this case the front of Roman buildings were expected to coincide with the line of Grantham Street.
Summer 1972	Broadgate	Small scale rescue work possible; examination of Sincil Dyke. Autumn–winter drill hall? Limited rescue work on the eastern defences of the lower colonia.
Winter 1972–3	Chapel Lane	Possibility of displaying colonia wall.
Spring 1973	St Paul in the Bail (Phase 2)	Medieval and Saxon levels?
Summer 1973	Silvergate, Saltergate	Rescue work again possible in Roman and medieval context.
Summer 1973	Steep Hill	Important site where street frontage of Roman and medieval dates should be located.
Winter 1973–4	Cathedral relief road	Rescue excavations along areas of possible Roman cemeteries, extra-mural buildings.
Spring 1974	St Paul in the Bail (Phase 3)	Roman levels.
Summer 1974	Inner relief road	Major Roman, Saxon and medieval rescue excavation along line of proposed relief road designed to cut off Lincoln conservation area no. 1 from the southern side of the city.

Source: Lincoln Archaeological Trust

subsequent settlement was twice the size of, for example, Gloucester's, because the upper colony had been extended from the original fortress area. The problem of working to a timetable accentuates the difficulties of the urban rescue archaeologist, and the first thing that altered at Lincoln was the redevelopment timetable as the actual building programmes were dropped back by four years or more. Likewise, some schemes, like the inner relief road, were postponed from immediate action. But the unpredictable timetable and the sheer scale of re-development envisaged remain the same.

While the upper colonia, the area of the original fortress, was already subject to conservation orders protecting the cathedral, the castle area and a zone of historic buildings between the two, by the end of the 1970s Lincoln was undergoing a massive change in layout of the lower colonia area.

The list of redevelopment sites and other proposals from Lincoln is as good an example as one could wish to find of modern urban change and its implications for rescue archaeology. The inner relief road at Lincoln may perhaps never be built, not least perhaps as a result of the pressure of conservationists fighting for medieval buildings. And the role of inflation must be recognised—many projects planned for the City of London were held up through lack of development finance in the inflationary period of the mid-1970s. But this means, of course, that many projects have been postponed and not cancelled.

Similarly, changes in social engineering threaten to make urban cores once again a very sensitive development area in the 1980s. Whereas much redevelopment in the 1960s and the 1970s was concerned with the peripheries of major towns in the form of inner relief roads and the like, subsequently there were moves towards the repopulation of derelict urban centres. Manchester provides a good example. The 1970s saw the inner population drop to less than a quarter of a million, even including the new occupants of the high rise flats in Hulme and Moss Side. Then, the very heart of the city began being re-colonised by urban housing projects, such as Deansgate in 1978. The excavations at Deansgate, continuing work from 1972, had uncovered a substantial area of the civilian settlement attached to the Roman fort long known to anti-quaries as Castle Field but submerged over a century ago by the tide of the Industrial Revolution. The consequent destruction and damage to the known site was thought to have put an end to the possibility of meaningful archaeology in the heartland of Manchester.

In fact this was far from being the case; instead, the focus had to be altered—away from the limited area of the military fort to the possible areas of associated civilian settlement. These settlements often dwarfed the actual military sites around which they had originally appeared, and can reflect the historical and social change of later Roman Britain

Fig. 6 Engraving of part of the Roman fort's south-east gateway (built over in the nineteenth century), Manchester

Fig. 7 Early second-century timber buildings excavated in the civilian settlement, Manchester 1978

far more accurately than the hulk of a barrack block. Thus the dismissal of Manchester's archaeological potential was a fallacy. When A. J. P. Taylor wrote that, 'Manchester had a Roman foundation though not worth lingering on. Its only standing structure remaining, a fragment of wall, in the goods yard at the bottom of Deansgate, must rank as the least interesting Roman remain in England, which is setting a high standard'. Until 1972 attention had been focused exclusively on the small area of the military fort, and the survival of plentiful archaeology in the civilian area a stone's throw away had been overlooked.

During the 1970s archaeologists also became increasingly skilled at recognising the remains of timber buildings. The possibility of work outside the fort therefore depended on the survival of intact levels or stratigraphy, as archaeologists call it, in areas undamaged by modern cellars and sewage systems. Fortunately, in Manchester the industrial core had expanded so quickly from being 'the largest village in Britain' that the early nineteenth-century buildings (unless they were pubs!) lacked cellars and substantial foundations. Under these conditions it was possible to recover the remains of timber buildings from as late a period as the fourth century AD, as well as better preserved examples from the second and third centuries. In such industrialised areas as the centre of Manchester, it was the absence of large medieval archaeological deposits and the speed of growth during the Industrial Revolution that in effect preserved the Roman levels to a substantial degree. The lack of foundations is a little-known advantage of rescue archaeology in the North. Similar situations were uncovered at Wallsend at the eastern end of Hadrian's Wall, and across the River Tyne at South Shields.

The work in Manchester was done by a team organised around the Department of Archaeology in the University. This, too, was part of the pattern of archaeology in the North where the increased archaeology budget of the late 1970s was spread thinly. The growth of active field units was initially limited to those at Chester and, later, York. Unfortunately the presence of a unit with salaried staff in a relatively under-financed area tends to restrict the response to other threatened archaeological sites, however pressing or academically important. The partial growth of excavation units in the North, therefore, was offset by the role of the universities with the expertise and some of the resources to maintain field teams as need arose. Archaeological units were established in association with the Universities of Manchester, Liverpool (run down in 1983) and Lancaster. Since the rapid changes of the 1970s fell short of creating the fully-fledged state archaeological service, the universities still have an important role to play. So, too, do the Royal Commissions. Much of the work of established units has been concerned with surveys of one kind or another. Yet it is the universities and the commissions that have the skilled staff best placed to record and assess county or larger areas. As inflation has bitten deeper into the newly-won rescue archaeology budget, so substantial savings could have been achieved by integrating the universities and commissions into the everyday work of rescue archaeology. Unlike the United States, where universities have been subcontracted by the federal agencies to work on large-scale rescue projects, in this country there has been a reluctance of the units to integrate active field archaeologists from the universities into longer-term programmes.

A partial reason for this lies in the creation of another body of archaeologists at county level. The creation of some independent excavation teams, whatever their precise titles, was a response to immediate needs in the late 1960s and early 1970s. Planners and archaeologists were brought face to face in many British towns. For example, at Lincoln the archaeologists' programme was controlled by the planners' redevelopment schemes as shown in Table 1 (p. 22).

But the area of contact extended far beyond the urban to the rural. The planning department of a medium-sized county, such as Somerset, receives something in the order of 13–16,000 planning applications a year. To deal with these, a number of county archaeologist posts have been established, normally within their relevant planning department. (Although the overwhelming majority of such applications have no relevance to archaeology or other environmental considerations, they nonetheless have to be sifted.) The earliest appointment was that of Ben Edwards to Lancashire County Council in the early 1960s. His task was not made easy: he was placed inappropriately within the Archive Department, and had to deal with two major city conurbations, Manchester and Liverpool, within what was then the county area.

But the lesson was learned, and 1973 saw the formation of an association of county archaeology officers with a membership covering most English counties. David Baker, Bedfordshire's representative, and first chairman of the new association, wrote in the County Council's *Gazette*, 'No local authority is obliged at present to become involved in field archaeology but about fifteen [now 26] counties have appointed archaeological officers, thus recognising that the subject is important enough to their overall responsibilities to require the employment of professional advisers.'

To illustrate the problem at the time, Table 2 lists archaeological sites involved in planning applications to Cheshire County Council during a single month in 1974, a year that saw major urban redevelopment. The possible threats were of varying natures. The laying of a major water supply main near to a known archaeological site requires a watching brief on the actual work, if the line of the pipe cannot be diverted: further important discoveries might be made during the

TABLE 2   The archaeological implications of planning applications to Cheshire County Council, January 1974

Prehistoric sites	*Threat*
1 Delamere: scheduled barrows at Seven Lows Farm	Laying of major water supply main
2 Betchton: site of Bronze Age burial unearthed in 1928	New buildings to be erected on land immediately adjoining site of 1928 discovery

Roman sites	
3 Tarvin Sands: Watling Street	New picnic site complex, etc.
4 Stamford Bridge to Saltersbridge: Watling Street	Major road works planned
5 Newbold Astbury: Bent Farm—Roman camp?	New building to be erected

Medieval and post-medieval sites	
6 Alderley Edge: moated site at Chorley Hall (Grade II* Listed Building, early 15th century and later)	New buildings and extensive drain laying within the moated area
7 Little Budworth: moated site	New buildings
8 Allostock: moated site at Hulme Hall (Grade I Listed Building, 14th century and later)	Drain laying, etc. within the moated area
9 Austerson: The Old Hall (Grade II* Listed Building, 15th century and later)	Demolition and removal of the building to new site
10 Wilmslow: Hawthorne Hall (Grade I Listed Building, 17th century)	New building and additions
11 Mottram St Andrews: Mottram Cross (medieval with later restorations)	Dismantling and removal of Cross to new site
12 Great Budworth: medieval core of village	Extensive sewerage schemes

Nantwich: medieval core	
13 Site at bottom of Mill Street	⎫
14 Gardens to 20–24 Barker Street	
15 Pillory Street: municipal car park	
16 Properties adjacent to Nantwich Bridge (also site of early ford)	
	⎬ *New distributor road*
17 Car parks to rear of The Crown Hotel, 16–24 High Street; 28 High Street; properties at bottom of Castle Street (site of Nantwich Castle and possible Roman brine workings)	⎭

Source: Archaeology Officer, Cheshire County Council

construction process and require urgent action. Many chance finds also occur during road works, particularly road widening, in archaeological zones or in medieval villages. Moated sites present another problem: the current building would probably be the successor to several others built within the same confines, and alterations are likely to uncover the remains of earlier buildings.

The new distributor road proposed for the medieval centre of Nantwich, presented special problems. Small sites were likely to be passed over because other larger sites either related to the site of an early ford or overlay the area known from documentary evidence to contain the medieval castle. The castle ditch is known to have been associated with brine production, an industry that, in this area, may have gone back to the Roman period. So in Nantwich there appeared to be a case for substantial rescue excavation which was forthcoming in the following year.

At this point in such a case the archaeologist is faced with the question of ways and means. With sufficient time, finance might be raised from the Department of the Environment to support a rescue programme. In addition, since local government reorganisation in 1974 the individual counties have become more involved, financially and otherwise, in the execution of field work. At that time there was a shift in thinking that placed some county archaeological officers, such as John Little of South Yorkshire and Phil Mayes of West Yorkshire in departments of recreation, leisure and health. This was, perhaps, an indicator of the way in which local government increasingly regarded rescue archaeology as lying in the field of recreation and culture.

Whatever the case, the link with planning applications means that there have to be close links with planning departments, where most of the appointments lie. Clearly, however, the appointment of one or two archaeology officers in planning departments of county councils was only the first of a series of possible steps. Another was the retention by the local authority of a permanent field team on its staff. This in fact subsequently took place in several counties, notably West Yorkshire, Bedfordshire and Essex, where teams were funded by a combination of support from their respective county councils and the Department of the Environment. It was in this context that, in May 1974, the Association of County Archaeological Officers welcomed the Department of the Environment's decision to establish a network of regional advisory committees (disestablished with other 'quangos' in 1979) to examine archaeology on the basis of selected regions forming coherent archaeological zones.

To summarise, the counties where arachaeology was more strongly organised had, by the mid-1970s, established varying degrees of competence in the field. This normally took the form of increased staff within the planning departments. To deal with *ad hoc* problems, outside experience was used, in the form of either temporary staff or, sometimes, assistance from the nearest university. Some counties, however, took a more fundamental step and established full-scale county excavation units. Table 3 shows two views of a small-sized archaeological unit: A, the structure of a small unit in local authority terms, and B, an archaeologists' view of an excavation project in operation under such a structure. Neither view excludes the other; they are simply different analyses of the same process. The wide spread of the necessary manpower is evident.

There are problems involved in setting up such units: subvention from industry or private benefaction to a local authority organisation are necessarily limited; and, once established, any archaeological unit requires its own offices and storage facilities, as well as, in some cases, a greater mobility than that provided by a single central base. In some areas the situation was to some extent pre-empted by the establishment of independent trusts to which the county council subscribed. The earliest and outstanding example of this was in Oxfordshire where the many archaeological interests combined to form a county-based trust with a central base and out-station offices. The establishment of a trust allowed the gravel extractors, Ameys, to make an annual subvention to rescue work along the Thames gravels (winning them the Rescue award of 1977), and at the same time gained the support of the Oxfordshire County Council.

By the late 1970s rescue archaeology was straining its financial limits to the extreme and fresh financial sources were being tapped. As a result, many archaeological units were relying for labour very extensively on the newly-formed Job Creation Schemes of the Manpower Services Commission that had become, by 1979, increasingly selective in their application. The employment of these schemes under a number of titles across the last decade has occurred against a background of the rising tide of unemployment. Their effectiveness for archaeology has come to depend on the care taken in the selection process and the provision of a high level of supervision, something that it has proved increasingly difficult to provide under the terms of the schemes.

TABLE 3 Roles in a small archaeological unit

A Unit organisation

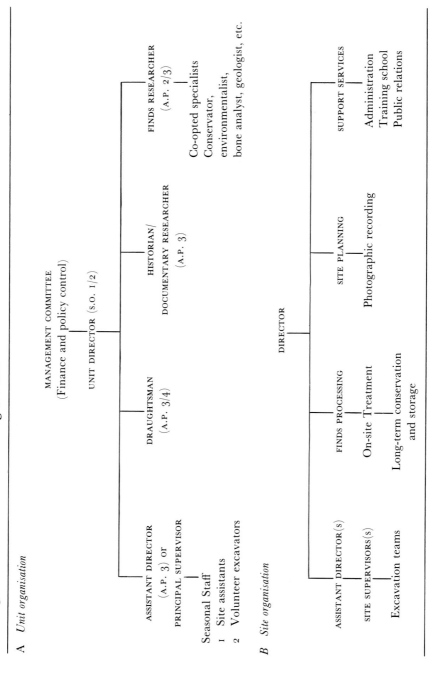

MANAGEMENT COMMITTEE
(Finance and policy control)

UNIT DIRECTOR (S.O. 1/2)

ASSISTANT DIRECTOR
(A.P. 3) or
PRINCIPAL SUPERVISOR

Seasonal Staff
1 Site assistants
2 Volunteer excavators

DRAUGHTSMAN
(A.P. 3/4)

HISTORIAN/
DOCUMENTARY RESEARCHER
(A.P. 3)

FINDS RESEARCHER
(A.P. 2/3)

Co-opted specialists
Conservator,
environmentalist,
bone analyst, geologist, etc.

B Site organisation

DIRECTOR

ASSISTANT DIRECTOR(s)

SITE SUPERVISORS(s)

Excavation teams

FINDS PROCESSING

On-site Treatment

Long-term conservation
and storage

SITE PLANNING

Photographic recording

SUPPORT SERVICES

Administration
Training school
Public relations

3
The Toothless Watchdog

Before the 1979 Ancient Monuments and Archaeological Areas Act, the framework for modern archaeology depended on a series of Acts going back to 1882 and modified in 1913, 1931 and 1953. It is perhaps symptomatic of the ambivalence of the British attitude towards archaeology that while the country's standing remains are amongst the envy of the world, there is, even now, insufficient legislation to prevent the archaeological destruction of urban sites by private developers; and, indeed, ineffective legislation to facilitate the excavation of key sites in the face of opposition from landowners. By way of contrast, as long ago as 1960 the Italian archaeological authorities adjudged the important eighth-century site of Santa Cornelia in the Roman Campagna to be in danger from annual ploughing. Despite opposition to excavation from the landowner-farmer, Italian legislation allowed the archaeological superintendency to place a ban on cultivation over the archaeological zone concerned. As a result a permit was granted for excavation—which was in fact to be carried out by foreign archaeologists! In Britain it was revealing that, in government legislation over Acknowledgement Payments, the Farmers' Union was extensively consulted during the committee stage, while the Council for British Archaeology, the government supported organisation for archaeology in this country, was not once asked for its opinion.

Scheduling and guardianship

What is the legislation? The Ancient Monuments Acts are meant to cover not simply upstanding monuments, such as castles and abbeys, but also the whole class of surviving remains known as field monuments. The overwhelming weight of current legislation is concerned with the countryside rather than the towns, although this situation ceased to reflect archaeological thinking from the early 1970s. In general terms the legal framework provides for a series of responses in the preservation of *individual* remains. The first and most common process is that known as scheduling. The term is applied to monuments that have been selected for their relative importance either in academic terms or in terms of their state of preservation. Scheduling is intended to impose a statutory period of three months for negotiation between the Inspectorate for Ancient Monuments of the Department of the Environment and any landowner intent on destroying or otherwise modifying a scheduled site.

The placing of a site or upstanding building under guardianship is altogether different. It enables the Department of the Environment to maintain and, if necessary, excavate the site concerned. Ultimately the Minister responsible through the Department of the Environment possesses the authority to prosecute anyone damaging a site under schedule or guardianship. As an emergency resort it is also possible to present an interim preservation order to protect the site that is under immediate threat of destruction. Most sites in guardianship in this country are upstanding buildings of national significance; by 1967, according to the Walsh Report, a government report, published in 1968, specifically designed to examine this problem, and the first and most thorough survey of its kind, 204 other field monuments were also protected by this arrangement, whereby the Department of the Environment is directly responsible for ownership and upkeep.

The great majority of sites, however, has always lain under scheduling arrangements. Although, theoretically, an owner gives three months' notice in the event of any threat, the procedure is as much honoured in the breach as the observance. Furthermore, over the years the Council for British Archaeology has consistently noted the reluctance to serve an interim preservation order which would constitute the Department of the Environment's next protective measure. This is because the serving of such an order involves compensation to the owner, who can in any case oppose such an action in a legal enquiry, and the findings might well be against the Department of the Environment: between 1927 and 1967 the order was served in only 20 instances, showing the reluctance in following this course of action, especially since the legal penalties are derisory.

The practical effects of this legislative framework have varied throughout the country. The Walsh Report concluded from actual results in the field that 'in many respects [they] fall markedly short of what could be obtainable'. At the then Minister's request the Report had included the results of a survey of 640 field monuments in Wiltshire: of these over 250 were found to have been severely damaged or actually destroyed, while a further 150 had suffered damage to a lesser extent. These figures were produced by the Department of the Environment's own Inspectors, and show the failure of the framework in practical terms.

The acceptance of ploughing as an inevitable part of normal cultivation has meant that this framework is at its least effective in relation to heavily arable or afforested land, for example, in the East Midlands and the Highland Zone, or in marginal areas where government agricultural policy has spawned financial incentives for the creation of additional arable land, for example, in Wales and the South West. In the 1960s shallow depth was defined by the Ministry of Agriculture as eight to nine inches (20 to 23 centimetres), so that mechanical ploughing has been highly destructive to buried sites: in fact most modern ploughing has affected levels considerably deeper. As a principle in rescue excavation, however, this was only recognised in a limited number of cases as late as the 1970s, for example at Whitton (Glamorganshire), Chalton Down (Hampshire) and Gussage All Saints (Dorset).

By the end of the 1960s it had already been felt that something had to be done to slow down the process of erosion. As one of its major points, the Walsh Report had specifically recommended that a star system should be developed within scheduling, between the categories of scheduling and guardianship, to identify the more important scheduled sites. The recommendation was an attempt to bring greater security to scheduled monuments that were particularly worth preserving for academic and historic reasons. The Report calculated that in a sample area of Wiltshire, of 720 scheduled sites, 117 merited inclusion in the starred category, representing approximately 18 per cent of scheduled sites in one of England's richest archaeological areas. Applied nationally, some 2,000 of the 16,000 scheduled sites might have required starring. Yet the scheme was specifically rejected by the government at the committee stage of the Field Monuments Bill of 1972.

The only piece of legislation that passed through parliament to implement one of the recommendations of the Walsh Report established the practice of Acknowledgement Payments to landowners with scheduled monuments in their possession. The resulting compensation (a farmer derived £20 to £30 a year for the presence of a scheduled barrow on his land) is perhaps less important than the establishment of the principle of financial payment to offset the restrictions that archaeology places on agricultural operations: it is analogous with compensation paid by the Central Electricity Board for the erection of power cables across the countryside. The most effective use of the Acknowledgement Payments system could well be in its application to a number of important or typical areas within which the whole archaeological environment would be preserved.

Unfortunately, the individualised nature of scheduling and the character of modern agricultural development combine to hinder the intended provisions of the legislation. This is evident from examples of the effects of scheduling on the ground. The field monuments in an area of downland in Wessex, another of Britain's rich archaeological zones, set a high standard of preservation. The plan (Fig. 8) centres on the neolithic causewayed camp at Whitesheet Hill in Wiltshire. One of the

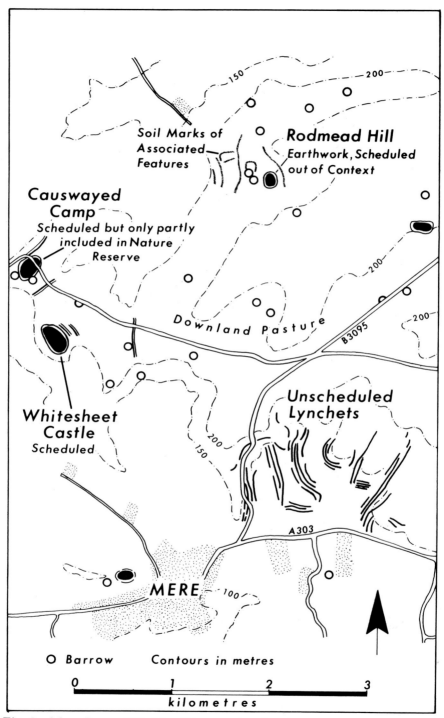

Soil Marks of
Associated
Features

Rodmead Hill
Earthwork, Scheduled
out of Context

Causwayed
Camp
Scheduled but only partly
included in Nature
Reserve

Downland Pasture

B3095

Unscheduled
Lynchets

Whitesheet
Castle
Scheduled

A 303

MERE

O Barrow   Contours in metres

0   1   2   3

kilometres

Fig. 8   Mere Down, Wiltshire. Diagram showing the very varied protection of
field monuments by scheduling

later barrows lies astride the ditch. To the east there is a hill-fort with its associated dykes across the ridges. A modern reservoir lies alongside the hill-fort. The hill-fort and causewayed camp are scheduled monuments, and the good state of conservation is a direct result of the fact that the farmer-landowner has chosen to concentrate on sheep and cattle-grazing rather than on arable farming. It must be emphasised that relatively unploughed areas containing a number of archaeological remains in which the major items are scheduled are increasingly rare in downland areas such as this.

The problem of isolated scheduling is brought out most clearly in the northern part of the plan. The earthwork at Rodmead Hill is scheduled, and, as a result, preserved as a grass-grown area amid the arable land. Yet air photography shows that the arable contains traces of enclosures and ditches directly associated with the central scheduled nucleus. Thus, while some scheduling is better than none at all, greater care is needed in defining archaeologically sensitive areas comprising major and minor features of the same complex, or areas of archaeological remains, of which part survives as a visible upstanding feature, whilst the rest has been abraded below ground level.

The *reductio ad absurdum* of the scheduling process is reached when only the banks of a hill-fort or other earthwork are subject to a scheduling order.

Credon Hill camp in Herefordshire was the scene of an important excavation in the late 1960s that uncovered remains of rectangular houses in the interior. Yet only the outer rampart is scheduled, while the interior is given over to afforestation. Far worse is the situation at Sutton Walls, north of Hereford. The hill-fort was re-used by King Offa during his campaigns against the Welsh, but only the ramparts are scheduled. Toxic industrial waste was dumped in the unscheduled interior of the earthwork, and has, on one occasion, spontaneously ignited. Clearly this is an extreme case, but it serves to emphasise the importance of protecting the interior of such sites for ultimate archaeological investigation. Such protection is particularly important when there has been re-use, such as, for instance, at Cadbury, where excavation in the late 1960s confirmed the tradition of Dark Age occupation, and at Eddisbury in Cheshire, a northern hill-fort, that is known to have been the site of a Saxon burh.

Plough damage

Unfortunately scheduling alone is not necessarily adequate physical protection for an archaeological entity. A few years of ploughing can effectively destroy a barrow and even scheduled examples frequently suffer from ploughing up to the edge of the visible mound, which destroys the perimeter ditches. One of the most alarming statistics that promoted the formation of Rescue was the rate of destruction of such round barrows. Dorset abounds with examples of the consequences of this process: by the late 1960s in South Dorset, for instance, less than 10 per cent of the 871 recorded round barrows remained undamaged, and since then more have suffered. In Gloucestershire over half of the 360 known round barrows, scheduled and unscheduled, have been destroyed, and there exists only one surviving barrow cemetery.

The process of destruction can be seen throughout the downlands of southern Britain, even, on occasion, in the case of scheduled monuments. If aerial photography or observation on the ground after ploughing shows dark patches in the centre of the barrow disc, indicating that the chalk capping has been abraded, this means, in archaeological terms, that the central core, incorporating the primary burial, has been destroyed (see Fig. 9). Ploughing around the barrow perimeter carries away the secondary burials. Figure 9 shows the process of destruction in stages. The scheduling of isolated examples of barrows is little answer to a fundamental problem which requires at least the strict conservation of a number of such archaeological environments

Fig. 9 The destruction of barrows: (a) the upstanding mound, partly protected by trees; (b) the trees have been removed and ploughing has eaten into the central mound and the surrounding ditch; (c) agricultural activity has almost entirely destroyed the mound; (d) virtually nothing remains—only the ploughed down white marks indicate the position of the barrow

(a)

(b)

(c)

(d)

Fig. 10 A Roman villa, seven miles north of Chelmsford, the remains of which appeared during the drought of 1975–6. Its shape shows clearly but the structural remains have been affected by each year's ploughing. The technique of aerial photography constantly reveals such examples of newly discovered sites to the archaeological record

prior to their ultimate destruction through the increasingly effective mechanisation of British farming.

Farming operations are likely to damage the known or partially known archaeological remains of field monuments. There is always the possibility that the ploughing of fields that have been under permanent pasture for a considerable period will produce fresh archaeological evidence: in fields that have not been actively cultivated for some considerable time ploughing often reveals the remains of the underlying features by producing differential soil marks. Likewise the banks or ditches of a site may be on such a scale, even in ploughed down form, that the farmer, without necessarily understanding what he is dealing with, decides to level them mechanically. (Indeed the scale of earthworks is often such that *archaeologists* do not understand them to their full extent.)

Levelling by machine inevitably destroys the archaeological content of the earthworks, but this is a drastic form of action and most farming operations are on a smaller scale, although even these are likely to have archaeological implications. The removal of field boundaries is a commonplace occurrence but it is important to remember that some have historical origins, in places dating back to the medieval period and beyond. Many hedgerows follow parish boundaries or reflect the line of Roman roads or later lane systems. Furthermore, hedgerows may mask a linear feature such as Offa's Dyke. Indeed the removal of hedgerows along its neighbour, Wat's Dyke, meant that two miles of its length have simply disappeared as far as the observer on the ground is concerned.

Periodic deep ploughing which cuts into the subsoil below normal depths is also relatively common. While it sometimes serves to locate unknown features, as in the ploughing of permanent pasture, it is also destructive: by this means many Celtic field-systems of the chalk downlands—Mere Down is a classic example—have been both revealed and steadily destroyed. The cutting of drains can also destroy archaeological features. On a large scale the removal of peat poses a similar threat which, however, can be avoided as, for example, on the Somerset Levels. There from the late 1960s onwards, extensive co-operation with the developers has led to considerable excavation of prehistoric trackways. Another aspect of agricultural improvement is the removal of copses and small woodlands, many of which contain remains of some kind. The removal of tree roots and replanting are naturally destructive and, as in the case of Danebury hill-fort, major excavations may be necessary as a rescue project in the face of uprooting and replanting.

Since farms are often the direct successors of medieval or even earlier settlements, one farm may form, for instance, the present-day visible remains of a deserted medieval village and the greatest cause of destruction is likely to be new building or reconstruction near a farm itself. Changing agricultural practices and other improvements often mean that new farm buildings, especially silos, are constructed alongside older buildings, or that the actual farmhouse is rebuilt nearby. In the north of the country, particularly in the Pennines, many of the upstanding Roman sites were re-used as defensive enclaves and ultimately farms and farm structures were built either inside or attached to their enclosures. Such sites inevitably contain deep archaeological deposits and there are associated remains on the outside because many *vici* or civilian settlements, that may be more important and extensive than their parent sites, grew up around them. Thus, for instance, by 1978 the construction of new storage barns at the fort sites of Bewcastle and Old Penrith in Cumbria had led to the need for substantial rescue excavations, respectively in the interior and around the periphery of these fort sites. And at Low Burrow Bridge, not far away, farm extensions revealed the site of the bath-house of the Roman fort. Some farm developments would not have been allowed if archaeological interests had been taken into account. Figure 11 shows Killyberry Rings near Weybridge where, in the 1970s, half an important and completely

Fig. 11   Killyberry Rings near Weybridge, Cornwall. The concentric banks visible on the right have been flattened by ploughing on the left. The farm buildings have progressively eaten into the interior

unexplored site was first ploughed out and then barns were built across a quarter of the interior.

Afforestation

The problem of unknown sites is that, although they may be antici-pated, they cannot be precisely located until destruction is taking place. The Forestry Commission owns a larger area of Britain than any other authority, and private forestry companies such as the Economic Forestry Group, Fountain Forestry Ltd and Tilhill Forestry (Scotland) also operate over very extensive areas, particularly in Scotland. The attitude of the Commission and indeed of most of the private concerns has been co-operative and informed, especially following initiatives by Rescue in 1974–5: very few known sites are destroyed or damaged in new projects, and the problem centres on previously unknown remains.

The twin Tine Plough, affecting a depth between 0.5 and 0.70 metres, and the Clark Trailing Plough, used in the initial ground-breaking operation for drainage and cutting as deep as 0.9 metres can be archaeologically very destructive. Moreover the lateral effect of the larger ploughs is as great as 1.7 metres, thus rendering disturbance very

Fig. 12 Forestry encroaching on a hill-fort, Bury Walls, near Clun, Shropshire

extensive wherever ploughing occurs. A single furrow can effectively destroy the stone core of an upland cairn, and quite legally, since for the forestry company employee the only archaeological site is a known and scheduled one. In a sample survey of 1975 in Dumfries, of 144 listed sites only 34 were found to be scheduled.

While the Forestry Commission trains personnel to recognise archaeological remains, the onus of locating new sites and making others aware of their existence remains with the archaeologists. This process must operate at two levels: at local level there is a great shortage of archaeologists (particularly in Scotland); at the national level there needs to be a far greater willingness if not to schedule then otherwise to protect, the substantial number of upland sites known in areas that are likely to be affected by afforestation schemes (northern Scotland is a constant example). Detailed and skilled archaeological survey fully supported by aerial photography and other aids should be a prerequisite of any new afforestation scheme. And much progress was made along these lines in Scotland by the late 1970s.

Re-afforestation of a specialised kind allowed large-scale work to be undertaken at Danebury during the 1970s, and the excavation of approximately one third of this major Wessex hill-fort illustrates the problems posed by afforestation and the imaginative archaeological solutions that can be found. Lying inaccessible beneath a dense beech wood a few miles north of Stockbridge, Danebury hill-fort was acquired by Hampshire County Council in 1968 with the aim of incorporating the archaeological remains (suitably interpreted for the public) into a countryside park. Professor Barry Cunliffe's first season of excavation revealed not only the great archaeological potential but also a major environmental problem: the beech trees were starting to die rapidly from beech bark necrosis, and this also presented a safety hazard. While the planners decided to maintain the tree-cover on the hilltop, it was decided that, as each area was cleared of dead or dying trees, it should be excavated archaeologically before any replanting took place. The entrance was amongst the first of such areas to be excavated, so that, after back-filling, a timber corduroy could be laid to protect the site from the wear of heavy forestry vehicles.

Over a decade the excavations produced a previously little suspected picture of an interior: internal roadways were flanked by planned rows of houses in their hundreds and with their associated rubbish pits; and puzzling practices such as the dismemberment of human corpses were revealed. The overall planning on a large scale allowed insights into the ways in which a structured society was organised and controlled during several centuries in the later Iron Age. Excavations in the mid-1970s by Stan Stanford, extra-mural tutor at Birmingham University, at Croft Ambrey in the Welsh March showed that such results are not likely to be uncommon from a late Iron Age site.

Treasure hunting

The enormous growth of what is euphemistically termed 'treasure hunting', or the detection of metal objects beneath the surface of the ground, has been totally antipathetic to archaeology. It is possible to use metal detectors responsibly on excavations to predetermine the position of metalwork and so ensure a higher standard of excavation. However, in almost every case the use of such machines has lain in the recovery of metal, principally coins, for pleasure, in what has been enticingly termed a 'leisure activity', but also, more especially, for gain. In behaving in this way, 'enthusiasts', as the treasure hunters' magazine has called them, have violated the growing concept of Britain's archaeological heritage as a finite and non-renewable resource.

On the many occasions that have all too infrequently received publicity, the person using a metal detector has committed damage on a scheduled site without knowing it. Further legislative reform could see the establishment of an easily recognisable symbol for scheduled monuments so that ignorance could not be claimed as an excuse for 'treasure hunting'. Under the 1979 Act interference by a person using a

Fig. 13 The destructive results of metal detection. The holes left after illicit digging are visible in the foreground of a site at Stansted, Essex

metal-detector in a monument is an offence. Examples of interference with scheduled sites have been legion, and many of the newer and more expensive machines claim increasingly deep powers of detection and selectivity. For instance, the newest type of machine was used by a party of oil men in north-east Scotland on a medieval religious site near Elgin where their delving for coins in the sandy subsoil left a series of deep pits in the statutorily protected site. Although the scene was monitored and reported to the Inspectorate, no action or prosecution followed. And the hunt for objects located by machines operating at only a shallow depth can be just as damaging in archaeological terms: delving into the top few centimetres of a site can affect the highly sensitive uppermost layers, such as happened at the important hill-fort of Uleybury in the Cotswolds. Excavation of these layers is most difficult and their interpretation, for example, the late re-occupation of a hill-fort, is of particular interest. By scooping out an object such as a coin from the back of a rampart the treasure-hunter, knowingly or otherwise, removes that object from its true context in stratigraphic terms; but he is also stealing the evidence that the archaeologist can use to set the surviving features in context.

Context is very important. Even in the more understandable case of using a metal detector on a beach or foreshore, it is little use recovering a single ancient coin, whatever its intrinsic interest, unless its associated material, whether further coins or pottery, is also located to make some sense of the group in terms of date or function. Many treasure hunters claim that they are aware of such factors, that they do not interfere with scheduled sites; and that they obey a code of conduct that is acceptable to archaeology. This may well be true for some practitioners, perhaps even for a majority, but case after case offers evidence to the contrary. In 1979 there were scandalous instances of treasure hunting: one leading practitioner was apprehended by the police digging at night in a scheduled area at the site of Old Sarum outside Salisbury; and a few weeks earlier a hoard of 60,000 coins had been found at the Roman site of Mildenhall by metal detection, and probably came from the scheduled area.

Whatever the semantic gloss conveyed by the words 'pastime' or 'leisure activity', there can be little doubt that financial gain is the dominating incentive for treasure hunters. Unfortunately Treasure Trove legislation, by its very name, promotes this attitude. The emphasis is on the recovery of gold or silver objects for which, if openly declared, the finder receives a reward. The origins of this legislation lie in a medieval law whereby the Crown sought to increase the royal coffers. The finds are Treasure Trove and belong to the Crown in the guise of the British Museum or its equivalents in Scotland and Wales. The criterion applied in designating Treasure Trove is the possibility of the depositor's return to reclaim his possessions—a reasonable presumption in the case of a coin hoard but less so in the case of other items. Unfortunately the existing system favours the national museums which are thereby ensured of a supply of the most valuable finds and see little cause to alter the arrangements. In Scotland, however, where slightly different legislation operates, the context of the find receives somewhat more attention: Treasure Trove is extended to include, not only gold and silver, but also other metals such as copper and bronze, and indeed other items like shale and jet ornaments. This definition at least goes some way towards keeping the group of finds together as a whole, and thus towards assessing its date and history. The famous Water Newton hoard of early Christian silverware is a particular case in point. If its immediate archaeological context had been recovered or its position plotted with sufficient accuracy, eventual excavation might have set the discovery in the context of an actual house or even of a small church within the Roman town of Durobrivae.

A real underlying difficulty rests in the fact that any discussion of Treasure Trove is limited to what is openly declared. The amount of valuable archaeological material that is illicitly sold in Britain cannot be quantified. The export market is very lucrative in the United States, where bronze axe-heads, for example, are much in demand, and there is a flourishing trade in such items from the gravel quarries of the Thames Valley and in East Anglia. Although in Britain there is not as yet anything like the organised and, at times, violent, clandestine operations of the illegal export of antiquities from Turkey and Italy, the results of such individual initiative or profiteering as does exist is nonetheless an appreciable and increasing erosion of a material heritage.

In the areas discussed there is at least some legislative provision for safeguarding archaeological remains or providing an opportunity for archaeological work to take place. The protection afforded may, at times, be unsatisfactory or slender, but at least it exists on paper. It could indeed be argued that there is satisfactory archaeological legislation in Britain, if it were only applied firmly and consistently. In the last decade, for instance, the Department of the Environment has brought a mere handful of prosecutions for damage or defacement of scheduled ancient monuments. In any event, the penalties are likely to be derisory, but at least a prosecution gains publicity and can have a deterrent effect, particularly, it is to be hoped, among treasure-hunting groups.

Urban development
The legislation that does exist relates exclusively to field monuments, and, therefore, only to the countryside. The claims of urban archaeology, the greatest single area of growth in rescue archaeology, are completely overlooked in legal terms. There exists no statutory process, save a few designated areas, such as parts of the core at York, whereby the claims of archaeological remains known (or reasonably presumed) to underlie a development area, can be recognised.

Access is all-important. Guaranteed access in a redevelopment programme is the only basis on which the forward financial planning necessary in undertaking excavations can be carried out. In cities such as York and London, where a large archaeological unit working in urban conditions needs to be able to plan its staff's activities for months, even years, ahead, such access is essential. But unless the local authority takes a favourable view of archaeology it is not automatic: several local authorities have viewed archaeological excavations with apprehension or have acted obstructively.

As archaeology has been brought increasingly into the corporate planning process, such cases have become rarer, but this does not apply in the private field. A clause in the working conditions recommended by the Royal Institute of British Architects simply urged anyone making a find on a building site (and this refers to pottery or other material rather than the remains of structures in the ground) to hand the material to the site architect or engineer.

All fossils, antiquities, and other objects of interest or value which may be found on the site or in excavating the same during the progress of the Works shall become the property of the Employer, and upon discovery of such an object the Contractor shall forthwith:

(a)   Use his best endeavours not to disturb the object and shall cease work if and insofar as the continuance of work would endanger the object or prevent or impede its excavation or its removal;

(b)   Take all steps which may be necessary to preserve the object in the exact position and condition in which it was found, and

(c)   Inform the Architect/Supervising Officer or the Clerk of Works of the discovery and precise location of the object.

The underlying attitude is that archaeology may be satisfied by handing over bits and pieces of pottery while work is actually in progress. In reality the archaeologist is overwhelmingly anxious to avoid the confrontation situation of operating alongside a contractor; and as some contractors are beginning to realise, an archaeological excavation can be beneficial to them in the preparation of a subsoil for building, especially when it is pitted with wells and rubbish pits.

The subject has unfortunately been confused in many developers' minds by the discovery of the temple of Mithras in the City of London in the 1950s. Public interest was such that the developer eventually generously took up the temple and rebuilt it in the outside patio of the new office block. However, the unforeseen problem caused by the discovery and its importance doubtlessly involved some delay, and time means money in the construction industry. Thus, although the discovery of the temple and its splendid statuary made a great impact at the time, and in fact the actual removal of the Mithraeum and its reconstruction only cost £5,500, the temple of Mithras is often cited by developers as a reason for not granting access to a redevelopment site and for taking a hostile attitude towards rescue excavation.

Besides the problems of the private development sector there can also be formidable difficulties within local authorities, all the worse for occurring at a level that precludes public debate. Often these stem from interdepartmental conflicts or the relatively junior status of the archaeological officer within a planning department, as occurred in a case that became the basis for a Private Member's Bill in 1971. Officers and other interested parties held a meeting concerning the construction of a new building in a major historical city. Rescue excavation prior to construction was in financial difficulty but had shown that the developer's soil tests had underestimated the effect of the less compacted archaeological deposits which, in places, reached to depths of over three metres down to bedrock and marked the remains of a tower concealed in the core of the city wall to one side of the site.

The Inspector of the Department of the Environment was prepared to offer very little, if any, money, although laying great stress on the importance of the dig. After talks with the structural engineer the chief planner stated that the cost of extras in foundations for a comprehensive dig six metres (20 feet) deep would be in the region of £20–30,000, which the inspector thought was a reasonable amount to be met by the developing authority! A discussion on the reservation of land adjacent to the Roman wall followed.

> The Archaeologist queried the proximity of the new building to the supposed line of the Roman wall, the Architect stated that it would be useful to know the line of the wall as soon as possible although not essential.
>
> After much fruitless discussion including the usual resignation threats and moral obligation sermons from the Archaeologists (as at the meeting held three weeks previously) it was agreed that the dig is only to be extended in the following ways:–
>
> 1. The existing L-shaped holes to only be made 2 ft deeper. No new holes to be started until either money is made available for the extra costs in foundations by the Department of the Environment, or the developer agrees to subsidise the Archaeologists to this extent.
> 2. Three exploratory holes may be made alongside the Roman Wall for location purposes.

The notable element in the record of this debate is that the attack on the archaeological officer was an internal attack made by another member of the same planning department. The archaeologists had in fact shown that previous estimates of the load-bearing capacity of the subsoil required revision and, in doing so, had saved the developing authority considerable further expense that would have resulted from alterations to foundation plans. How different is the situation in Scandinavia where a percentage of the costs of examining the underlying archaeological remains has to be borne by the developer, and concealment of material of historical or archaeological interest is an offence.

The developer

Yet the greatest difficulties in obtaining access for rescue excavation generally occur in the private sector. In 1974 a typical example occurred in Perth, a royal burgh that was once the capital of Scotland, and therefore a prime candidate for archaeological investigation. During a redevelopment project in the High Street, the axis of the medieval city, the examination of nearby drainage and foundation trenches proved that archaeological deposits did exist to a considerable extent and that no excavation had taken place to date. The laying of drains to a neighbouring restaurant had shown that the subsoil contained not merely stratified levels but also organic deposits, where the degree of survival of such items as food, leather and clothing would be high. The site in question contained only limited cellarage so that it was certain to yield results to excavation.

The Secretary of the Perth Civic Trust raised the question of the archaeological potential of the site with the contractors, requesting access for a brief period for professional archaeological examination immediately after demolition. After a dilatory correspondence with the contractors and clients, culminating in a refusal at a date too late for any other action, the Secretary wrote to her MP outlining the case, and he, in turn, could do no more than write to the Minister of State and 'get the Government's reaction to the position' since a 'matter of principle' was involved':

> As you may know, [A] have acquired the site of the 'old' post office in Perth High Street. The post office building had been demolished and the Perth Civic Trust hoped that it might be possible for some archaeological investigation to be made before the new building starts.
>
> The reason for this is that the site was in the centre of medieval Perth, and it is possible that valuable evidence of the medieval buildings on the line of the High Street may lie beneath the old post office.
>
> In the correspondence that has taken place, I note that [B, the construction firm] expressed the view (through their Divisional Manager) that it was doubtful that sufficient time would be available between the completion of demolition and the commencement of new works for any archaeological exploration. In a further letter earlier this month, [B] stated that they were not carrying out any 'deep' excavation, and would doubt that any archaeological findings of interest would be made. Last week, [A] informed the Hon. Secretary of the Civic Trust that, following discussions with their various experts, they would not be able to comply with the Perth Civic Trust's wishes.
>
> Of course, it may be impossible from the time point of view to allow any archaeological survey to take place on the site. But in view of the need to seize any opportunity to explore the little that remains of the medieval town, it does seem a great pity that some archaeological exploration could not be arranged . . .

In this case, after several months and much correspondence, nothing was achieved from the archaeological standpoint, despite the fact that the original request for excavation facilities for a brief period had been commuted to simple access for observation by persons who were adequately insured and professionally competent. In one of her letters the Secretary of the Civic Trust made a number of points which are still, unfortunately, relevant.

> . . . a change of attitude is needed from firms such as these who move in from outside to redevelop sites in our medieval cities.
>
> I know that pressure has been growing recently in England from groups

such as 'Rescue' (in liaison with the Council for British Archaeology) but here in Scotland the situation is much less satisfactory. We need a much more enlightened outlook, not only on the part of private developers but also from local authorities. I understand that the latter can, if they wish, make planning consent dependent on time being allowed for archaeological investigations to take place before redevelopment. And, of course, the local authority should also allow time for this when doing their own redeveloping. However, until we have legislation which makes this obligatory we shall have to depend on the goodwill of the planning departments and shall just have to continue to try to persuade them to take the needs of archaeology into consideration when considering planning applications.

The reply sympathetically informed the Secretary that 'if the developer cannot be persuaded to allow time for archaeological examination of a site no powers exist to compel him' and 'it is more than likely that a solution will require legislation and it is not possible to say when and if that will be enacted.'

It is a sad story with literally hundreds of parallels up and down the country that are rarely brought to the public's notice. But, only a few weeks later, an article was published describing the forthcoming redevelopment of large areas of the same High Street (*Perthshire Advertiser*, 27th July 1974), so that, once again, Perth was faced with a major archaeological opportunity. Closer to the River Tay there was evidence to suggest that the organic deposit lay deeper, and, far more important, the location of land in Parliament Close was thought, as the name suggests, to mark the site of a Scottish Parliament building, close to the presumed site of the Royal castle (in the area of the present museum) alongside the river.

This second redevelopment site was undoubtedly more important than the first: it related to an historically documented site of major importance in Scotland's past. Yet at the end of 1974 there was still no indication that the site would receive adequate archaeological investigation prior to redevelopment. That it did so eventually was due to outside as well as local pressure, but equally to a sympathetic developer, Marks & Spencer, who actually postponed construction once the archaeological richness of the site was confirmed. The firm even instilled some good sense into its birth pangs: the unrealistically low salary proposed for the incoming archaeological director was neatly scotched by the firm's representative as well below that paid to their secretaries! Thanks to the goodwill of a sympathetic and intelligent private developer, Perth High Street excavations were ultimately a success story and an important factor in the upsurge in Scottish urban archaeology in the 1970s (p. 115).

4
Capital rescue

In terms of improvement, whether financial, legal, or otherwise, in the 1970s British archaeology faced the fundamental question of whether the whole is more important than the parts: were archaeologists prepared to press for improvements for their profession as a whole at the occasional risk of affecting their own personal positions? Inevitably any attempts at structural alteration tended to be made in the face of the Department of the Environment. This body is responsible for administering the Ancient Monuments Acts as they currently stand, whether or not it agrees with them. Yet, as often as not, progress is made by conflict. Some archaeologists have shunned contention as beyond the realm of the academic; some simply keep silence to ensure continuity of finance from the Department of the Environment for their own excavations. Some have stayed silent and hoped that the efforts of others would bring improvements which they could then say would have happened in any case. Some simply regarded contact with 'the mechanics of opinion formation' in the modern world as in some way unbecoming. In addition, the sense of euphoria which the summer digging season always seems to bring to the archaeological world, focuses attention on the individual site rather than on long-term overall problems, the solution of which lies *outside* the field of archaeology.

Indeed, with so many powerful characters in the world of archaeology it is strange that, unlike trades unions and, in more recent years, many environmental bodies, archaeologists have not previously sought support in parliamentary lobbying. The protracted failure to rewrite either the financial or the legislative basis of archaeology in the late 1950s and the 1960s led directly to the eruption of change in the 1970s. Little enough money came from central government sources; even though funding by the Department of the Environment rose from £210,000 in 1970 to over £1,000,000 by 1980, the sum still compared unfavourably with that spent in other European countries. At the start of the 1970s the Dutch spent more than 30 times as much per head of population on archaeology as the British, and the Swedes 48 times as much. Archaeologists were frustrated since sites were ill-protected compared with those in Scandinavia, where contractors are prosecuted for failure to report archaeological finds made during construction and where planning permission for buildings is dependent on a satisfactory report from a qualified archaeologist. It was distress at the lack of this kind of official concern in Britain and a spate of reports pointing to the bleak conclusion that, unless something was done immediately, this country's archaeological future would be permanently imperilled, that led to the formation of the Rescue Trust for British Archaeology in 1971, and the rejuvenation of the Council for British Archaeology as a major propagandist force.

In the 1960s the Council had largely fulfilled a role as a clearing-house for information. Indeed its dependence on financial support from central government made its use impossible as a vehicle for substantial improvement. Professor Charles Thomas, its President in the early 1970s, was well aware of this fact, and he and the Secretary, Peter Fowler of Bristol University, accordingly embarked on a programme of publication in the areas of fieldwork and rescue archaeology. The main result in the latter field was the publication of *The Erosion of History*.

Thomas and Fowler joined with other archaeologists in two important meetings. At the first, a meeting of extra-mural tutors, Barrie Long of Manchester, a specialist in systems analysis who had become involved in rescue archaeology through this author's excavations in his home town of Carmarthen, posed the archaeologists a question: what could they expect to achieve if they remained so disorganised and failed to recognise that improvement in the overall condition of rescue archaeology could only be achieved by applying methods and pressures from non-archaeological sources? This led ultimately to two meetings of a ginger group, at Barford in Warwickshire, and at Newcastle, and the start of the rescue movement as a pioneering environmental pressure group.

In large part rescue archaeology is about people: the success or failure of a scheme so often depends, not on archaeological factors, but on the ability, determination or pure bloody-mindedness of an individual in impressing his proposals on others and implementing them effectively. Time and again the individual archaeologist, even though he realised that most of his problems of implementation lay in the non-archaeological field, has plunged into the all-consuming problems of *his* site. Rarely does he stop to extrapolate what is applicable nationally: amongst academics excavation and anarchy go hand in hand. It was a very significant turn of events, therefore, when in 1971, a group of younger archaeologists, dismayed by the lack of progress in the cause of rescue work at a period of unprecedented opportunity, saw that the only solution lay in a national campaign, and that the only way to improve the provisions for an academic discipline lay often in non-academic action.

This was the impetus that sparked the creation of Rescue. In many ways its earliest days were also its most difficult. A meeting of invited archaeologists at Barford, Warwickshire, heard a series of cogent short papers designed to paint an entirely new picture of what should be done for rescue archaeology in Britain. Such was the dissatisfaction amongst professional archaeologists that in 1970 and 1971 there was no difficulty in raising the largest audiences in London that British archaeology had ever known. Yet the picture of Elysium with 50 to 100,000 members of Rescue, though preached with zeal, had the effect of inducing scepticism amongst professionals. To the older generation, moreover, with distinguished academic careers, pressure on a national scale was, if not anathema, still something they simply had not contemplated.

Philip Barker's messianic zeal was better directed at the public in general than at a cynical audience of professionals. Martin Biddle, the first chairman of Rescue, had a straightforward message: on the basis of European parallels, of which he was supremely aware, Britain was in a situation infinitely inferior to that in Holland, Germany, Denmark or Italy. But British archaeologists were reluctant to think regionally, let alone nationally, and this was exactly what they were being asked to do. The grass roots reaction was that the key to archaeological work is the parish—'to think in national terms you must think you're God or a professor!' In the bureaucratic area it was one of near total hostility: the Inspectorate within the Department of the Environment had never before had to face such fundamental criticism and it did not command the facts about either state archaeological services abroad or the disbursements of its own finances. Moreover the Chief Inspector at the time was fundamentally opposed to pressing for revised legislation within the Department of the Environment, albeit that the Walsh Report of 1968, however little concerned with urban rescue work, read as a standing indictment of current legislation surrounding the destruction of field monuments. The Walsh Report had been firmly tucked on the shelf, ignored save in one respect, the introduction of Acknowledgement Payments for the preservation of scheduled sites, which was put into effect by the government of 1971–4 (p. 33).

The effect of the launch of Rescue was, therefore, twofold. There was general agreement that 'something had to be done', but also deep antipathy in some quarters. Membership dropped away with the erosion of idealism at the end of its first year. The reasons were multifarious. There were the inevitable criticisms that its officers were self-seeking, that it was élitist, ineffectual or interfering, the latter description particularly used to justify its rejection by Scottish archaeologists in 1971. There were also inherent dangers in its structure: a generation in archaeology is probably as little as eight to ten years, and many of the everyday 'dirt archaeologists' regarded some of the members of the Rescue committee as old hat. Rescue also took a novel turn in electing to reduce overheads by establishing its office at Worcester alongside Philip Barker's extra-mural base; although half the committee meetings were held in London, the effect of meetings in Worcester was, in some eyes, to shroud them with mystery. Yet the decision to make Worcester the main centre was a clear indication that Rescue's executive was not to be bound by the London nexus.

Valid criticism probably centred on failure to do something for the regions. Rescue's system of regional officers rarely worked effectively, but on the other hand the organisation has always preferred to use its limited fighting fund to act as a catalyst through 'implication surveys' and the like, rather than directly financing excavation. Its greatest successes stem from its role as an independent pressure group, but one that has its support resting on a broad membership.

Yet critics and protagonists alike expected too much. If the number of members originally hoped for was illusory, then the critics failed to face up to the problems of launching a body that inevitably had to seek membership in the general public, outside the archaeological sphere. Public enthusiasm had to be raised, not for the particular site in the High Street, but for rescue archaeology on a national scale and particularly in areas such as the North West, where there was little public awareness anyway, and, inevitably, donations from the business world for the general rather than the particular are slim. Despite its difficult tasks, in the threefold fields of operation amongst archaeologists, central and local government, and public opinion, Rescue can probably claim two areas of success. Significantly it is perhaps in the first-mentioned that acceptance was slowest.

The Rescue Committee was fortunate in having two members from the business world with the time and will to participate. One was Robert Kiln, a Lloyd's broker who, in the early 1970s, master-minded the creation of the first effective insurance scheme for excavations. Himself a keen excavator in Hertfordshire, he has never forgotten the volunteers who do the actual work. The other businessman was Graham Thomas, and time and again the two were able to cut through the haze of good intentions and convince archaeologists that, if anything was to be achieved, Rescue, like so many other charities at the time, had to operate at a professional level in public relations and fund-raising. With the help of a professional public relations officer a campaign was launched in local government offices, professional bodies, industry and government. *The Erosion of History* was introduced at the Town Planning Institute's conference where its views were overwhelmingly endorsed. Industry was approached both for support, as a result of which Lloyd's Bank, for example, sponsored excavations at York and Lincoln where their redevelopment sites were involved, and, above all, to sponsor

Rescue scholarships intended to train new archaeologists in the multiple techniques of modern rescue work.

Rescue worked on the basis that every local authority should ultimately have an archaeologist at its disposal to vet planning applications. In many ways the future of rescue archaeology lies with local government. This is partly because of the speed with which it can mobilise local support, as occurred as early as 1972 at Tewkesbury when the borough authority provided buildings for a Research Unit, hired an archaeologist for five months (and subsequently made the appointment permanent), and worked with Rescue in producing a contingency survey to pinpoint the archaeological potential of the redevelopment process within the town.

This approach was, however, anathema to the more establishment-minded archaeologists, particularly those based in London. The controversy was not perhaps one of aims but of method. Some officials of the Department of the Environment privately described the Rescue movement as a 'jobs for the boys' organisation, since sites and jobs were required to employ the increasing number of archaeological graduates produced by the universities. It was odd to hear Whitehall quoting Parkinson's Law, although in fact few of the original members of the Rescue Committee were directly concerned with the teaching of a university undergraduate course.

It is in the realm of public education that the rescue archaeology movement can really claim to have made progress during the 1970s. To a certain extent influencing the general public and stirring parliamentary interest went hand in hand. This is partly because the issues raised with the public ended up literally on MPs' own doorstep with the scandalous 'non-event' of New Palace Yard, Westminster. It was a lengthy development, crucial to the growth of rescue archaeology in the decade.

By the beginning of 1972 Graham Arnold, the Public Relations Officer then employed by the Rescue Trust, had created a situation the like of which had never before been seen in British archaeology. Archaeology was news; and literally hundreds of articles, good, bad and indifferent, abounded in the press. While this was a welcome change, there remained the problem of deepening the issues discussed, of moving beyond the object-oriented reportage of work in progress towards explanation of the underlying organisational, legal and financial problems. Fortunately, a series of events in 1972 coincided to bring this about. That they did so was made possible by the interest of several journalists: Patricia Connor of *The Sunday Times*, Richard Walter of *The Observer*, and Martin Walker and Norman Hammond, archaeology correspondents for *The Guardian* and *The Times* respectively. As Graham Arnold emphasised, however great the interest in archaeology at King's

Lynn or Kenilworth, nothing would actually be improved until there was an issue in the nation's capital, and, extraordinarily, the period from March 1972 to February 1973 provided three such issues.

On 26th March 1972 a major row exploded between archaeologists and the City of London Corporation over the lack of facilities to excavate the remains of Baynard's Castle on the City waterfront in the face of redevelopment. There was no doubt of the site's historical importance. The Castle stood at the south-west corner of the City close to present-day Blackfriar's Bridge. Founded in the Norman period, it had played a prominent role in English history: Henry VII refurbished the building; three of Henry VIII's wives had lived there; Mary was proclaimed Queen there and Shakespeare set part of Richard III there. The ruins were covered by riverside warehouses after the destruction of the Castle by the Great Fire of 1666.

In a frantic race against time to recover some information, Peter Marsden of the Guildhall Museum salvaged sufficient to show the layout of five waterfront towers and the massive south-western mult-angular tower. Ultimately he was given more time, and further infor-mation, particularly of organic remains from the harbour quay, was forthcoming. The excavation in 1974–6 at Trig Lane, immediately to the east, uncovered medieval and Roman waterfronts that could only have been thought to have survived following the investigation of the Baynard's Castle site.

If the successful result of these excavations was the creation of an Urban Excavation Unit under the direction of Brian Hobley from

Fig. 14   The excavation site of Baynard's Castle, London, 1972

Coventry Museum, it was the Baynard's Castle affair that revealed the ethical issues at their most stark. At the time the contribution of the City of London to facilitate excavation of archaeological sites prior to redevelopment was a little over £4,000, rather less than was then provided in Lincoln. 'There is no other city in the country where the dictates of money can override everything else,' claimed Martin Biddle. He was arguing that recalcitrant councils should be compelled by law to phase archaeological investigation into redevelopment schemes on historic sites of this kind, particularly as the intrusion of archaeological excavation adds only about one per cent to the development costs involved. The Guildhall Museum, with one field officer responsible for all sites in the City, was simply inadequate to cope with the problem. Under-financed and with insufficient access to planning programmes, it could not hope to represent the claims of archaeology effectively in planning committees. Above all, it lacked legal teeth to obtain access. a point that emerged clearly in the parliamentary questions that were provoked by the Baynard's Castle débâcle.

In the following month the argument was carried a stage further over the redevelopment of Leadenhall Market which overlies the massive Roman basilica and forum. It formed the focus of the ancient city, combining the functions of town hall, law courts and business centre. While it was clear that redevelopment of some kind was in train, conflicting accounts were emerging from the City Architect's Department, and official requests from the City's own archaeologists had not been answered, although one of the persons concerned had actually seen the plans informally.

The Market dated from 1881, and in 1972 it was still awaiting listing as an historic building, a rating that would have prevented demolition without prior notification to the Department of the Environment. But even this device would have been inadequate. The listing of a single building unit that bears only a partial relationship to the underlying remains cannot bring a satisfactory solution. The only answer lies in the realm of area scheduling within built-up areas, a legal device that would ensure long-term notice of development plans.

This was just one of the points raised in parliamentary questions put to Peter Walker, then Secretary of State for the Environment. What these questions also revealed was that the City of London's record in this matter was wholly behind the requirements of the time. *The Erosion of History* revealed that £4,500 had been contributed to rescue work in 1971–2, or 2.2 per cent of a penny rate, figures that contrasted with 32 per cent for Exeter and 50.9 per cent for Winchester. Any increase in finance, of course, would have been unjustified if it had not brought vastly improved organisation and facilities in its train. Outside archaeologists had long realised that the Guildhall Museum was unfortunately lacking in the structure necessary to cope with the potential for rescue work in the City, and, in the light of the Baynard's Castle and Leadenhall Market issues, Rescue pressed for the formation of an appropriately staffed rescue unit for the City of London along with an overhaul of the vetting of planning procedures.

As part of that programme there appeared, one year later, *The Future of London's Past*, written for Rescue by Martin Biddle, Daphne Hudson and Carolyn Heighway. A survey of the potential left within the City, it predicted what would be the major areas of destruction and redevelopment during the following decade. The book set a new standard of its kind and became compulsory reading for property developers (and two scholarships were created on the strength of it!). But its real achievement was to prompt, with considerable support from the Guildhall Museum and its Director, the creation of an Urban Archaeology Unit with a budget that rose to approximately £80,000 in two years, almost doubling the 1971–2 figure.

By this stage it had become clear that the press was becoming a formative power in the world of rescue archaeology. For instance, in the summer of 1972, the fledgling archaeological unit at York, which had just been established under the direction of Peter Addyman, was starved of funds by cutbacks by the Department of the Environment that threatened to suspend all excavation in that city. The picture was also reflected nationally in last-minute cutbacks that slowed or cancelled work, for example on the Kenilworth bypass. But a concerted effort to publicise the situation both in the press and on television had an effect: Mr Geoffrey Rippon announced an influx of funds for rescue work that, in particular, allowed the York project to survive its first summer.

The scene remained relatively quiet for several months. In 1972 MPs had approved the construction of an underground car park in Westminster's New Palace Yard, and in February 1973, work began with the news that the structure would cost £2.2 million or the equivalent of £4,500 per car. It became clear from investigative reporting by Martin Walker of *The Guardian* that the decision by the Department of the Environment to begin excavating the MPs' car park had been taken without reference to the Department's own archaeological section. The Chief Inspector said that he had made no statement to the Minister of Housing and Construction on the subject. Curiously, the Minister, then Mr Paul Channon, claimed that no warning of archaeological implications had been received regarding the site.

The mechanical gutting of the site—rapidly up-graded to the status of a watching brief—appeared to be in direct contravention of the Government's policy on the careful investigation necessary on major sites. The Department, while recommending that private developers

Fig. 15 New Palace Yard, Westminster. The controversial sight of cranes at work on the construction of an underground car park in 1973. The development destroyed remains dating back to the Saxon period without allowing proper examination, and led to a public outcry

allow and encourage pre-development archaeological investigation, had failed to act on its own principles in its own backyard. In an earlier reply to an MP's query, the Minister had claimed that an excavation would only be justified 'if we had really important and closely defined archaeological objectives in view'. Yet the possible objectives in view were the court of the Star Chamber, the eleventh-century palace of Edward the Confessor, and, conceivably, an underlying pre-Conquest palace or its outbuildings. All this information was readily available in the Department of the Environment's own magisterial publication, *The History of the King's Works* (HMSO, 1963, Vol. I, p. 492 ff.). As recently as the previous 5th December, Mr Channon had enunciated his policy in the Commons: 'If the monument or site is sufficiently important, there are powers to prevent the development. Otherwise it is the Government's practice to arrange an archaeological investigation so that the monument or site can be recorded before the development takes place.' No such prior investigation took place in New Palace Yard and the Department of the Environment's archaeological role was limited initially to a watching brief. Yet anyone with the most elementary knowledge of modern archaeology's interpretive achievements would have realised that the great majority of early features on the site might have belonged to timber structures that require area excavation to recover their plan. There is, however, reason to believe that substantial timber structures were encountered and that work was actually stopped for a period, at a monetary cost in standing-time approaching five figures—all under the cloak of secrecy.

The public debate continued for over a week in the press and other media, while the Minister and the Department's representatives dismissed the problem as the proverbial 'storm in a tea cup', or avoided it by questioning the arguments about location. It is instructive to survey the whole debate from the first enthusiastic reports of the discovery of a fifteenth-century fountain to the sudden realisation that fundamental principles were being flouted.

The Evening Standard 7.2.73
    Picture of work on uncovering fountain in New Palace Yard.
The Guardian 7.2.73
    Report of find of fountain in New Palace Yard by Ian Aitken, Political Correspondent—whole report in glowing terms for skill of Department of the Environment.
Eastern Evening News 8.2.73
    Glowing report on discovery of fountain.
Morning Star 10.2.73
    Picture of fountain—brief and enthusiastic caption.
Scotsman 10.2.73
    Fairly detailed comment on the discovery of the fountain, the preservation

of which is 'proving something of a headache for the Department of the Environment'.

Then came the realisation that a major opportunity for scientific excavation was being missed, and that the Department of the Environment was breaking the very rules it sought to impose on private developers.

The Guardian 13.2.73
'Canute may stem MPs' car park'—front page article on greater significance of New Palace Yard site with full references to *The History of the King's Works*.

The Guardian 14.2.73
'Star Chamber trial for Rippon'—the application of a 'watching brief' was 'a complete reversal of all archaeological principles' (Martin Biddle, Rescue's Chairman); 'How in hell can we rebuke private developers and local authorities for not preserving their archaeology when Parliament sets this kind of example?' (Tam Dalyell, MP).

The Guardian 15.2.73
'Department "broke its own ruling"'—'This decision so stunned archaeologists that they are convinced it must have been taken by administrators, and not by the Department's archaeologists.'

The Guardian 16.2.73
'Labour joins the lobby for Canute'—Mr Crosland was to take up the issue; Peter Fowler also added his authority to the mounting concern of historians and archaeologists. The European campaign to halt work on the car park was developing. Martin Biddle, was writing to all prominent European archaeologists, asking them to add the weight of their protest to the telegrams and letters of their British colleagues.

The Spectator 17.2.73
'Parliamentary vandals'—'It is difficult to think of any English site more worthy of archaeological investigation and, thereafter, preservation. It is also difficult to think of any modern purpose at all which could possibly justify the destruction now taking place.'

The Guardian 17.2.73
'Dig in the ribs'—'The fact that history's loss is the motorised MPs' gain is beginning to stir many Members' guilt feelings.' Need voiced for more money to be spent on archaeology, and for more effective legislation to be introduced. Possibility that a Private Member's Bill would be introduced which would insist on penalties for developers destroying important sites.

The Observer 18.2.73
General review of the situation, with both sides putting their cases. The disruption was seen by Martin Biddle as 'clear vindication of Rescue's campaign for a government archaeological service whose director would have an influential voice high in the Department's secretariat'.

The Guardian 22.2.73
Report on MPs' reaction to written reply by Paul Channon to Tam Dalyell's question: 'the statement is an exercise in misinformation'

(Martin Biddle). 'How can you find remains of wooden buildings hundreds of years old in a trench gouged out by a bulldozer?' (Peter Fowler). The handling of the car park situation threw gloom over a meeting to be held between rescue archaeologists and the Department: 'the government has done little to convince the archaeologists of its good faith.'

The Guardian 23.2.73

Letter from members of the History Department, University of Manchester, concerning the mishandling of the New Palace Yard situation.

The cause was, however, lost. As a palliative, the fifteenth-century fountain was disinterred for eventual re-erection. Months later the Minister announced that it had in fact overlain the remains of an earlier twelfth-century marble fountain, perhaps of the time of Henry II, proving the point about stratigraphy that archaeologists had been making all along.

Yet in another sense Westminster New Palace Yard was a victory for rescue archaeology. It was the first time that there had ever been a prolonged debate in the press about the legal principles shaping the practice of rescue archaeology. Equally important was the effect on MPs: the noise of mechanical excavators was clearly audible within the House of Commons to remind members that 'history's loss is the motorised MPs' gain'. It was clear that in a dramatic and immediate way the need to safeguard the future of buried archaeological deposits had at last come home to Westminster. The whole unfortunate affair of New Palace Yard convinced many MPs that Britain was the sick man of Europe in its governmental attitude towards archaeology, not simply financially but also in terms of legal restrictions on indiscriminate development of sites with archaeological potential.

5
Rural rides: motorways and New towns

While the affairs of Baynard's Castle and New Palace Yard were finally bringing home to MPs and others the problems facing rescue archaeology in Britain's cities, it was in the countryside that the battle of financial recognition was being won. Motorway archaeology was an aspect of rescue work that rapidly came of age in the 1970s, flourished and subsequently declined with the cutback in motorway building. That it came into being at all was in a large measure due to the organisation established by a single archaeologist, Peter Fowler, on the southern stretches of the M5.

Like gravel diggings, motorways are a mixed blessing to archaeology: their ultimate effect is, of course, wholly destructive, but during the period of construction there is a brief phase in the removal of topsoil that gives an opportunity for the recording of unknown sites on an arbitrary line normally some 60 metres across. Preliminary survey prior to the actual construction process is therefore a vital element, if meaningful results are to be obtained. The success of such a project relates directly to the efficiency of the regional archaeologists, and, sadly, across Britain as a whole those motorways that have received any archaeological survey have been in the minority. Yet where work was done, particularly in the South West, the results have brought a quantitative revolution in our knowledge of the density of rural settlement. In an often-quoted statistic, over the 100-mile section of the M5 between Worcestershire and the southern border of Somerset only two archaeological sites were known prior to road construction; during the course of that construction some 200 archaeological sites were located, that is, an average of approximately two sites per mile along what was, in archaeological terms, a purely arbitrary line.

Motorways

Recovery of information depends entirely upon the competence and speed of the archaeological teams assigned to each section of the motorway. The pioneer work on the M5 spawned other groups and committees to cope with the problems presented by the second generation of motorways, such as the M11 in East Anglia and the M40 in Oxfordshire. At the same time the climate of opinion in the

Fig. 16 Troutbeck, Cumbria, between Penrith and Keswick. A Roman marching camp can be seen in the centre. Like the adjacent fort (to the right), it was damaged by a trunk road improvement scheme which, as the figure shows, was fortunately diverted to the south

construction world was shifting, and it allowed archaeological considerations to be taken into account earlier in the route selection process. For example, preliminary investigations into the extension of the M15 motorway near Solihull suggested that more than 200 archaeological sites might be affected in some way.

By forward planning it is, of course, possible to select a route that will avoid destruction of the more important sites and so reduce to more manageable proportions the amount of rescue work required. Naturally enough, it is not possible to avoid destruction in every case. The problem lies in effectively integrating the processes of construction and investigation within the brief period available. So much of this depends on the personal relationship established between archaeologist and contractor, and, historically, this could have meant that such work would have been conducted under haphazard and downright hostile conditions. But, thanks largely to the initiative on the M5 and its effect on the construction press, contractors became increasingly helpful in granting access and at times lending equipment. In work at the Welwyn diversion of the A1M trunk road near Lymsford, for example, a clause

63

was actually included in the contract to ensure that Roman remains were not destroyed.

Although the M5 operation can now be seen to have been the starting-point for motorway archaeology in this country, it should not necessarily be looked on as a model because of the lack of long-term preparatory work and the pressures to which volunteer groups were at times subjected: the M5 operation is best seen, as Peter Fowler has suggested, as an example of the British archaeological tradition of muddling through and achieving some results despite all the odds. Yet the results were significant, not only academically, but also politically. They were sufficient for Lord Sandford, the government minister concerned, to make a special allocation of £100,000 extra funds in the early 1970s to enable the additional pressures of motorway archaeology to be catered for: along the M5 it was subsequently possible to organise teams of workers to conduct rescue excavations of the larger sites known to underlie the motorway route, notably Roman villas and other farm buildings along the fertile eastern side of the Severn Valley between Gloucester and Bristol.

The overall results of the M5 work are in many ways too extensive to synthesise here. It was perhaps the cumulative results that were most impressive, not simply because of the volume of sites recovered, but also because it became possible to assess the intensity of occupation at varying periods: for example, in contrast to the late prehistoric and early medieval periods, the Roman period is now known to rival the later medieval period in the density of settlement.

By the mid-1970s interest had turned away from the M5 and the M4 in the West, towards the projected lines of such routes as the M40 east of Oxford. The work on this stretch of motorway offers some detailed examples of the way in which the archaeologists were still forced to work. At Heath Farm, for instance, near Tetsworth, on the line of the projected motorway, a mere three days were allowed to tackle the excavation and recording of eight round huts and an associated field system found in the primary stripping of the route. This kind of last-minute activity would have been untypical of a programme that included much planned rescue excavation in addition to the inevitable salvage work carried out once a motorway route became known in detail. The salvage operation at Heath Farm was amongst a number of similar operations that provided some of the most important academic aspects of the work on the M40. It was the density of archaeological settlement that occasioned the greatest surprise, as it had done on the M5: extensive areas of prehistoric and Roman occupation were located near Tetsworth, an Anglo-Saxon cemetery was found at Postcombe and an important cemetery was also found alongside the Upper Icknield Way at Beacon Hill on the edge of a Chiltern escarpment. The woodland cover of the scarp edge had also concealed from prior discovery a medieval settlement that began life in the middle of the thirteenth century.

The work on the M40 provided important lessons in motorway archaeology. Among the problems the archaeologists faced were lack of money and recognition. However academically respectable and efficient, most motorway archaeology groups functioned with totally inadequate budgets that could be varied but took little account of the actual construction programme in the field. They relied therefore to a great extent on the self-sacrifice of individuals and the forbearance of farmers and contractors.

The M40 group suggested a solution: as a standard practice where archaeological work is involved in the early stages of a motorway contract, one-third of one per cent of a contract price should be set aside to allow for proper budgeting and forward planning. Such guaranteed finance makes a world of difference to the efficiency and productivity of an archaeological operation of this kind: such devices as the payment of compensation to farmers in advance allows access to key sites before the arrival of the bulldozer. This relatively modest proposal became a reality in the United States in 1975 with the result that any major redevelopment project there is statutorily required to contribute half a per cent of its overall budget to rescue archaeology.

Another motorway project, the proposed route of the M11 from the fringes of London towards Great Chesterford and Cambridge, set archaeologists a massive task of co-ordinated survey and excavation. Also in the eastern sector of the Home Counties, in East Hertfordshire, where the local society conducted a major excavation on an important cemetery site along the Puckeridge bypass on the A10, the main road from London to Cambridge, close co-operation with developers and contractors facilitated archaeological work. The contractors phased their work in such a way as to give excavators the maximum possible time. In return, working to a strict timetable, the archaeologists were able to cut the contractor's delays to a minimum. The burial groups recovered there are amongst the most important in the area and they varied from early cremation burials to third- and fourth-century inhumations cut into the flinty subsoil.

Recognition

There can be no doubt that the great professional and voluntary archaeological response to the upsurge in motorway building played a major part in affecting both governmental and public opinion in the 1970s. The major effect of the work on the M4 and M5 was recognised in a Parliamentary debate of 16th December 1971 (Hansard Vol. 326, No. 24, cols 1321–35):

Fig. 17 Grave goods excavated from a Roman cemetery, 1972, in advance of the construction of the Puckeridge bypass, Herts (Rescue)

There should be no need today, in 1971, to argue the case for the cultural importance of the work of archaeologists ... the first motorways to be subjected to anything approximating systematic archaeological search before and during their construction were the M4 and M5, where they pass through Wiltshire, Gloucestershire and Somerset ... The work was carried out by mixed amateur and professional teams operating on minimal budgets, but with the physical co-operation from day to day of the motorway construction unit and their contractors. No finance was available from motorway funds. The results of this effort were startling ... most of [the sites] were discovered only as a result of continuous observation—and I stress that word 'continuous' ... Motorways are being built at an increasing rate over the remainder of the country. It is impossible to expect the same superhuman efforts from people in these new areas. Additional finance is essential ... [Enthusiastic volunteers] are today carrying the great archaeological burden virtually unaided by the State.

(Viscount Hanworth)

There is no need to emphasise the growing interest in archaeology in this country. It is evidenced, for example ... by the large numbers of amateurs up and down the country who undertake incessant and invaluable voluntary work in this field.

(Lord Fletcher)

... those responsible for the planning and building of motorways are naturally fearful of the difficulties that may arise if archaeological discoveries are made on the line of their route. But these difficulties will be minimalised if an expert survey is carried out before work begins. In this way, requests for delay will be avoided ... Secondly, it is not always understood that archaeologists will only ask for the most significant discoveries to be preserved. For the most part, the essential thing is to have time to record the details of any discovery before it is destroyed ... once this work has been done, the destruction of the great majority of archaeological sites can be accepted as inevitable.

(Lord Hamilton of Dalzell)

Fig. 18 Skeleton with a repaired hip-fracture discovered during excavation in advance of the construction of the Puckeridge bypass (Rescue)

Fig. 19   Cley Hill, Warminster, Wiltshire. The needless destruction of part of a hill-fort by quarrying in the early years of the century

Fig. 20   The destruction of Moel Hiraddug hill-fort, Clwyd, by the siting of a limestone quarry at its northern end

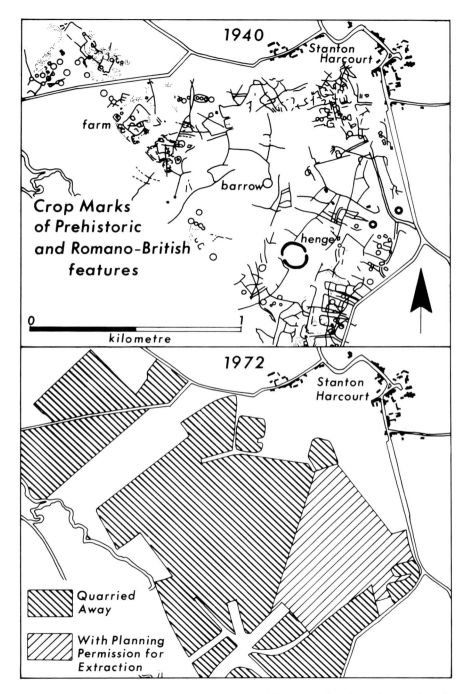

Within the figure (1940 map):
1940
Stanton Harcourt
farm
Crop Marks of Prehistoric and Romano-British features
barrow
henge
0   1
kilometre

(1972 map):
1972
Stanton Harcourt
Quarried Away
With Planning Permission for Extraction

Fig. 21 Stanton Harcourt, Oxfordshire. Diagram showing destruction by quarrying. The major part of the quarrying was carried out without planning permission for extraction

Although the volume of motorway construction began to decline in the mid-1970s important results were still forthcoming. Major rescue activities have been rare in the north of England but 1974 saw work carried out during the early phase of the new £7.8 million Hexham–Corbridge bypass. The 10-week archaeological rescue operation revealed the presence of a large Roman supply base constructed there at some time in the late first century AD, presumably as a base for northern campaigns, and prior to the construction of the well-known fort site a little to the east of Corbridge. The site engineers from Molem, the main contractors for the bypass, found remnants of pottery one mile to the west of Corbridge, in an area where Charles Daniels of Newcastle University had already excavated an apparently isolated bath-house some 20 years previously. He and John Gillam, also from Newcastle University, were taking a keen interest in the area, and identified the pottery as also belonging to the late first century AD, thus confirming suspicions that there might have been some form of Roman occupation in the area prior to the construction of Corstopitum fort.

A 2½-month project was involved in the delicate process of detecting the flimsy traces of timber buildings in the subsoil. Store buildings, workshops, possible barrack-blocks and stables were all identified, together with substantial areas given over to metal-working of some kind. The whole complex had been carefully dismantled by the Roman soldiers, and during the last days of the work the western defences were located giving some indication of the possible size of the base, the bulk of which now lies under farmland. Without the opportunity afforded by motorway building the site would have remained unknown.

Quarrying

Fortunately for archaeology generally the lessons of motorway archaeology were obvious to the public: important information could be recovered from this new kind of development in the landscape. It was not surprising therefore to find that other long-standing operations affecting the landscape were increasingly reviewed with fresh insight. Quarrying and gravel extraction are carried out on a very substantial scale in Britain. The siting of some of the older stone is unfortunate: much of the hill-fort at Breedon-on-the-Hill, north of Leicester, has been carved away by quarrying; the great hill-fort at Cley Hill near Longleat on the Wiltshire–Somerset border fell victim to the same process; and the northern end of the famous hill-fort at Moel Hiraddug in North Wales has been destroyed by a limestone quarry that could equally well have been sited on any one of a number of neighbouring outcrops formed from the same limestone bedrock but not crowned by a major archaeological monument. The most archaeologically destructive aspects of such quarries were largely checked in the 1970s through growing public pressure or official restrictions. But vigilance is still needed: in 1976 the interior of Ham Hill in Somerset, the largest hill-fort in Britain was reworked for stone. The operators were within their rights since their quarrying licence stemmed from the 1920s before the claims of archaeology had been properly formalised into the planning process.

By far the greatest change in attitude towards archaeology in the 1970s was caused, not by the extraction of hard rock, but by the quarrying of gravel. Most of the major river valleys, particularly in the East Midlands, are abundant sources of gravel, and, as air photography has shown, were also fertile areas of settlement for prehistoric man. The area of Stanton Harcourt on the Thames above Oxford showed a plan that revealed both a bewilderingly dense collection of crop marks (recorded by Major Allen during the 1930s) and the degree to which they have been destroyed in recent times. By the 1970s the story began to change, and in the face of such obvious forms of archaeological destruction increasing numbers of rescue excavations were mounted. In the case of the upper Thames, Ameys Ltd made substantial annual contributions to help the examination of sites being destroyed by their gravel-workings. At Mucking on the Essex shore of the Thames, excavation in advance of gravel-extraction was undertaken as a major project financed by the Department of the Environment. The work, carried out by Margaret Jones, produced a remarkable sequence of structures ranging from a Saxon settlement to an Iron Age village with

Fig. 22 Peat-cutting on the Somerset Levels, 1970

its land divisions overlooking the Thames foreshore, and the results constitute a remarkable testimony to what can be achieved by long-term rescue excavation.

Another example of progress by archaeologists working in co-operation with industry can be found on the Somerset Levels. There the traditional industry of peat-cutting is now carried out in a highly mechanised way by machines that can remove up to two metres of the topsoil. In this way a number of prehistoric timber-laced trackways were originally identified running across the Levels. In the 1960s a major rescue project with important research implications for the development of the prehistoric environment in the South West was being co-ordinated by John Coles of Cambridge University. The timber corduroys, such as the Sweet Track, acted as all-season trackways linking the small islands of the Levels, and date from as early as the third millenium BC. Apart from their intrinsic research interest, the conservation, publication and display of some of these timber trackways is a testimonial to co-operation between peat-extractors, the Department of the Environment Inspectorate and the archaeologist.

Plough damage

Peat extraction is perhaps a very specialised rescue threat. The greatest single destructive agent in the countryside, in the view of most archaeologists is modern ploughing. Although this is hard to prove because reliable statistics are difficult to obtain, the efficiency (and therefore depth) of modern ploughing, and in particular the growing use of chisel ploughs in subsoiling, were recognised in the 1970s as an important reason for rescue archaeology. (Regrettably this lesson was still far from satisfactorily learnt in the North of England.)

The realisation of the need for carefully selected rescue excavation in the face of persistent plough damge has led to some important archaeological discoveries. The annual destruction of the uppermost levels of the Roman villa at Whitton in the Vale of Glamorgan led the Welsh Inspectorate to launch a rescue excavation that uncovered the full building sequence on the site, from the circular timber huts of the pre-Roman phase to the rectangular stone-built structures of the later Roman period. In another pioneer operation members of Southampton University traced the remains of a Saxon village on Chalton Down, Hampshire. From the spread of fragmentary pottery in the ploughsoil, intensive field survey had established that an extensive site of the Saxon period probably lay undisturbed on the ridge at Chalton—undisturbed, that is, except by the effect of annual ploughing. In the face of promising evidence of the existence of a rural site untrammelled by later developments, the Department of the Environment's Inspectorate funded rescue excavation. This decision was dramatically vindicated

Fig. 23 Chalton Down, Hampshire. An aerial photograph showing the Saxon
village excavated while under the threat of plough damage (P. V. Addyman)
(inset shows a detail of this area)

Fig. 24 An aerial view of the late Iron Age farmstead excavated at Gussage All Saints, Dorset 1972

when, in successive seasons, the plan of a Saxon village emerged, making Chalton Down a type-site of its kind. Ploughing of the topsoil had destroyed the surface remains but, although much cut about by plough-marks, the chalk subsoil had retained the post-holes and construction trenches of the Saxon buildings. On the whole they exhibit rectangular plans, and the various building units share roughly the same axial alignment in this remarkable example of what can be achieved by rescue archaeology in a rural context.

The Inspectorate itself subsequently developed these initiatives in the Cranbourne Chase area, at the quaintly-named site of Gussage All Saints which provided a fuller picture of a late Iron Age farmstead than ever before. A similar large-scale operation saw the complete stripping of the henge monument at Mount Pleasant outside Dorchester, Dorset. Geoffrey Wainwright, then the Department's Inspector for the South West, worked at these two sites, and at the partial excavation of Durrington Walls in advance of road alterations north of Stonehenge. His experience made him an advocate of the establishment of a permanent skilled digging team within the Inspectorate to cope with rescue situations where there was no effective local workforce available.

The establishment of such a unit was in principle a considerable step forward, although in practice, the further the unit operated from its home base at Portsmouth, the more its operations appeared to have been carried out with little regard to cost effectiveness. Undoubtedly at a number of places, such as Shaugh Moor, a settlement complex on the western edge of Dartmoor, the existence of the excavation unit made possible year-round operations on a financial scale that would have been unthinkable in the 1960s. But even further substantial improvement was to hand, deriving not from these traditional problems of rural archaeology, but from an altogether new initiative: new towns were being planted in the countryside.

New towns

The annual report of a new town development corporation would normally be the last place to provide information about archaeological excavation and discovery. Yet in 1974 Northampton Development Corporation proudly announced the results of a series of important excavations within their area. The Development Corporation had already blazed the trail in 1973 with an independent publication of Iron Age sites excavated in the redevelopment area of Moulton Park and Blackthorn, the first full archaeological report to be published by any Development Corporation in the country.

Following this, the Corporation archaeologist, John Williams, excavated within Northampton itself. At St Peter Street in the old town centre important new information came to light, demonstrating the development of early Northampton. Beneath the modern levels lay a series of tanning pits of the sixteenth and seventeenth centuries, which in turn overlay two terraces of medieval stone houses, one of which contained two malt-roasting ovens of fourteenth- or fifteenth-century date. The structures appeared to have been of two storeys, and had suffered a common fate, being destroyed by fire in about AD 1500. This evidence corroborated documentation concerning a large fire occurring in the town in 1516. The houses were not in fact the first on the site: a street frontage pre-dating the Norman Conquest was also found, and in places as many as six superimposed structures were unravelled by the archaeological team. Still earlier building did not follow a set pattern, but comprised randomly placed houses and *grubenhausen* (sunken-floor dwellings) belonging to the tenth century. The earliest feature on the site was a ditch of Saxon or prehistoric date built to defend the area on which the church of St Peter now stands.

This outline of work at Northampton, embracing problems both rural and urban, illustrates the range of commitment that was to become a feature of new town development corporations, whereas ten years previously it had not even been contemplated. Northampton's close neighbour, Milton Keynes, comprises an area of 22,000 acres within which there are over 300 recorded archaeological sites dating from the

Bronze Age onwards, and including evidence of extensive Romano-British occupation, and obvious remains of the medieval period, not least of which are 15,000 acres of ridge and furrow.

Very few of these recorded archaeological sites are scheduled as Ancient Monuments. The inadequacy of this number shows the scale of the problem facing the town's archaeologists. Yet they do have certain advantages on their side. New town corporations generally possess an open, helpful outlook, reflecting the relative youth of the hundreds of planners on their staffs. The archaeologist, being a member incorporated within the planning structure, has automatic access to planning decisions at an early stage. There is therefore no reason why archaeological requirements cannot be built into the planning framework from the very beginning. Moreover, problems of access to sites disappear, since the corporation normally owns the land in question, or can lay down conditions for contractors prior to development. Additionally, development corporations normally pay a substantial part of the archaeological bills, and the provision of equipment and site offices is not a great problem within this context.

Situations such as this naturally presume a co-operative attitude towards archaeology among the controlling board of the development corporation as existed at Northampton in the case of the upper Nene Valley. At the other end of the valley, the Peterborough New Town Development Corporation has offered an equally impressive contribution towards rescue archaeology. In one of the most thorough redevelopment schemes in the country, the area of the Nene Valley to either side of Peterborough has been redeveloped. The city's expansion covers one of the richest archaeological areas in the country, and the programme of aerial photography and excavation has continued to reveal additional important discoveries. The centre of prehistoric interest lies at Fengate, to the east of the modern town. With the Roman invasion a legionary camp was established at Longthorpe to the west, and an auxiliary fort is known alongside the Roman equivalent of the Great North Road. This was the area in which the Roman potteries flourished around the village of Castor north of the Roman market town of Water Newton.

The Nene Valley constituted both the axis along which ancient settlements ran and the basis for the New Town plan. By 1972, although the pace of development had quickened, the archaeologists were by and large prepared: the Nene Valley had seen a great deal of work since the first threats to its sites with the widening of the A1 in 1957. Chris Taylor of the Royal Commission on Historical Monuments had published a survey of archaeological sites within the designated area of the New Town in 1969, and from the late 1960s, John Wild of Manchester University had been co-ordinating a series of rescue excavations with local assistance, until the increased pace of development necessitated the appointment, in 1972, of a full-time archaeological field officer. Donald Mackreth, the field officer, worked in collaboration with Adrian Challands, an archaeology officer appointed by the New Town Development Corporation itself.

In a remarkable initiative, the programme received help from an unexpected quarter, the Royal Ontario Museum of Toronto. Francis Pryor, one of the museum staff and a Cambridge graduate, brought in a team to tackle the many problems of the Fengate prehistoric site. It had become apparent that the small-scale exploratory trenching of previous years would provide no satisfactory solution for the working of this extensive and highly important neolithic site. Accordingly with the aid of mechanical stripping on a massive scale, acres of the Fengate complex were uncovered. The Museum's co-ordinated programme of total area clearance continued until 1978.

The importance of the Fengate site had been known from the early years of this century. The late G. Wyman Abbott had extracted a mass of material from what was probably the nucleus of the archaeological zone destroyed by gravel-quarrying prior to the First World War. Studies of the material, which came to be known as Peterborough ware, by both Abbott and other archaeologists were important for current knowledge of the later neolithic period. A truer picture of the actual extent of the site emerged more recently as a result of aerial photography and showed that settlement extended north-wards and north-eastwards from the quarrying site where it was first located.

Area-stripping on a large scale produced evidence from the late neolithic to the early Bronze Age. There were three detached settlements: one, the original quarrying site; the second comprised a rectangular enclosure; and the third, located in 1973, was formed by two rectilinear fields, apparently with entrances at every corner. The main occupation area, suggested by the amount of household refuse, lay within a ring ditch on the western side of the field system. Analysis of the wear on the edge of flint tools showed that the majority were used for butchering rather than scraping, and, from bone evidence, the animals concerned appeared to have been wild and domesticated ox. The predominant amount of cattle bones suggests that the settlement, set amid grassland with occasional patches of scrub, had been one in which the fields served as stock enclosures. Amidst the maze of ditches, particular attention focused on a rectangular arrangement, measuring some seven by eight-and-a-half metres, with substantial corner-posts, and some evidence for a central row of post-holes. These remains have been interpreted as the rare evidence of a primitive house—there is some suggestion of a hearth in close proximity. Radio-carbon dating of wood from the foundation trenches

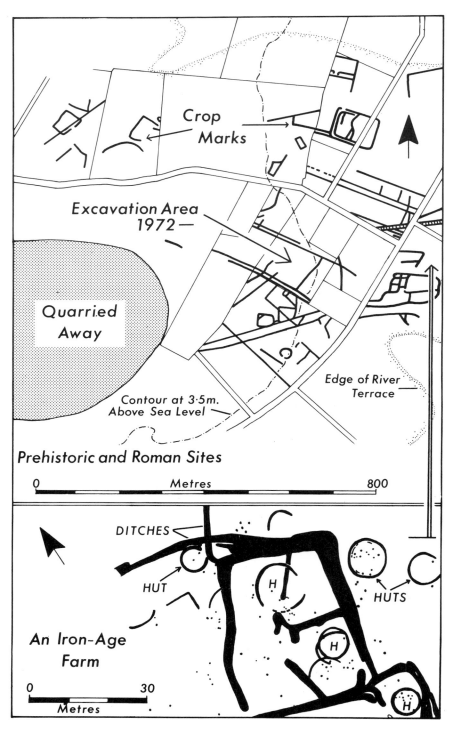

Crop
Marks

Excavation Area
1972—

Quarried
Away

Edge of River
Terrace

Contour at 3·5m.
Above Sea Level

Prehistoric and Roman Sites

0   Metres   800

DITCHES

HUT

HUTS

An Iron-Age
Farm

0   30
Metres

Fig. 25   Peterborough New Town. Diagram showing excavations at Fengate

pointed to a date round 3,000 BC. Pollen analysis suggests that it was built at a time of woodland clearance.

The pattern of settlement changed drastically in the Bronze Age, when the area of approximately one quarter of a mile square was largely given over to ditched enclosures associated with a number of possible settlement areas. The community concerned (which existed for approximately the last two centuries of the second millenium) seems to have been based primarily on the exploitation of livestock. An elementary system of transhumance may have been involved whereby the animals cropped the summer fodder available from the fenland islands, and moved westwards to the flood-free ground in the winter months.

The overall study of the agronomy of a neolithic to late Bronze Age settlement such as Fengate depends on an interlocking series of scientific tests, such as phosphate analysis, carbon-14 dating and flint examination. To this must be added sieving and flotation techniques. More important, however, is the overall, or macro, approach. There is still criticism that too much rescue excavation is carried out without specific aims, that is without being formulated in terms of question and answer. While there may be some validity in this argument, prehistoric sites such as Fengate overwhelmingly stand against it. Even though many of its features may have been apparent from crop markings, without total excavation none of the detailed evidence illustrating the development of the three different settlement patterns, and their respective economies, would have materialised. As a result of the scale of this unique foreign intervention in British archaeology, we have information at two levels: first, the actual details of the settlement area itself—the micro-settlement patterns—across a two-millenia timespan; and secondly, evidence that places the site in its larger prehistoric context, that is its ecological relationship with the edge of the fens—its exploitation of the nearby fen islands at Whittlesey, Eye and Oxney.

6
A Tale of Four Cities

The growth of urban rescue archaeology during the 1970s, involving relationships between archaeologists, redevelopment, planning and local authorities, as well as government expenditure, can be traced by examining our major historic towns in Britain. The scale of achievement reflects both the relative success of archaeologists in projecting archaeology as an environmental issue, and the positive response from local authorities.

Lincoln

With the foundation of a new archaeological trust for the city of Lincoln in April 1972, there was general hope that the level of emergency excavation would begin to keep pace with the major redevelopment programme scheduled for the city. The implications of the programme (see Table 1, p. 22) meant that excavation was called for across some $4\frac{3}{4}$ acres of the central core in the years 1973–4. Yet until 1973 when there were major provisions of staff and excavation funds, this would have been a task for which existing facilities were almost wholly inadequate, despite the fact that Lincoln has exceptional claims for archaeological attention. It is a city with many upstanding remains of great historic interest which are supported by documentary evidence. It was the base of a legion in the early years of the Roman invasion, and the fortress was subsequently turned into a *colonia*. This was subsequently more than doubled in size by the creation of a lower walled town running down to the River Witham so that the walled area within which archaeological finds could be confidently predicted was much greater.

In the 1950s work had concentrated on sections cut through the defences of the legionary fortress and upper *colonia*. The well-known Newport Arch forming the north gate of the *colonia* could not be examined extensively, but, in the 1960s, excavation on the east gate of the fortress (through the co-operation of Trust Houses Ltd), showed the prospective richness of the deposits. These revealed the transition from fortress to *colonia*, and thence into the medieval period. While this excavation was conducted for the City Museum by Ben Whitwell, by the early 1970s the pressure for rescue excavation had necessitated the

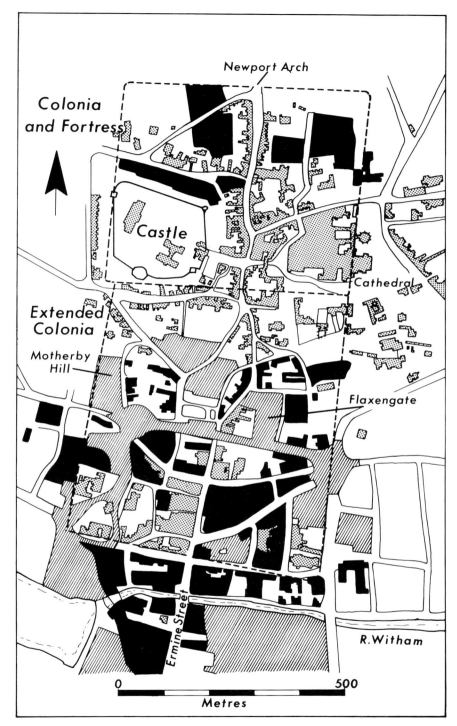

Labels on map: Newport Arch; Colonia and Fortress; Castle; Extended Colonia; Motherby Hill; Cathedral; Flaxengate; Ermine Street; R. Witham; 0 — 500 Metres

Fig. 26 Lincoln. Diagrammatic plan of principal sites and development schemes

development of separate excavational facilities supplied by the Lincoln Archaeological Trust under a newly-appointed director, Christina Colyer.

Much of the early work of the new unit concentrated on the western defences of the lower *colonia* on Motherby Hill in advance of the construction of a new divisional police headquarters. Such were the below-ground complexities of the site in relation to the proposed new building that it raised a fundamental question concerning compensation: should developers be compensated not so much for archaeological delays as for the instabilities in the subsoil uncovered by excavation and thereafter necessitating alterations to construction plans? A Private Member's Bill on this issue was unsuccessfully mooted in Parliament by Dick Taverne, the city's MP at the time. During emergency work in advance of new corporation buildings, the west gate was located a little way down the lower western defences. The defences of the extended *colonia* date to the second century AD, but were refurbished in the late fourth century. The gateway contained much re-used material and dated to the mid-fourth century, when it had replaced an earlier interval tower. The whole complex stood up to the remarkable height of 4.60 metres.

By 1973 the gaps in archaeological knowledge were obvious; there had so far been little excavation of medieval Lincoln. That year saw the beginning of an important series of excavations on medieval sites within the lower *colonia*. Medieval Lincoln also spread south of the Witham along the line of the High Street, close to the railway station, and exploratory work there showed a remarkable sequence of Roman and medieval buildings, suggesting that this southern area was of greater archaeological significance than had previously been thought. Work in 1973–4 was particularly concerned with the examination of medieval structures in the Flaxengate area within the lower *colonia*, an opportunity provided by the projected construction of an inner ring road. Documentary evidence suggested that wealthy merchants had lived in that area during the thirteenth century and their dwellings were found to have survived in the form of several thirteenth-century houses discovered in a surprisingly well-preserved condition. The houses with stone walls, clay floors, hearths and internal partitions, fronted on to Grantham Street and Flaxengate.

As the work of excavation advanced, the earlier remains of the Flaxengate site were uncovered, including those relating to the immediately post-Norman period. During the eleventh and early twelfth centuries buildings on the site had been mainly confined to one side of the road frontage and were recognised more by the remains of superimposed clay floors than by walls which had by then been largely robbed away. The timber buildings were generally rectilinear in plan and had been replaced by stone-built equivalents in the second half of the twelfth century. Their remains attested to the fact that there had been a considerable degree of prosperity in the twelfth and thirteenth centuries. The buildings revealed the classic pattern known from the ancient world; commercial use at ground-floor level and domestic accommodation to the rear and on the first storey. The principal evidence of commerce pointed to brewing and weaving, and it may be that these trades had been responsible for the prosperity of this area of the town. A similar standard of living and a very similar development sequence was also encountered in excavation at Broadgate, outside the walled area, in the medieval suburb known as Butwerk.

By this stage the pressure on the archaeologists was becoming desperate. The early years of the 1970s represented the worst period of structural recycling within the central core of Lincoln. If all the possible sites had been excavated, the total budget would have been un-paralleled in any one city for any one year. The very richness of Lincoln's archaeological heritage meant that some of the claims of rescue archaeology had to be ignored, and in the event many potential sites had to be discarded. Even so, in 1973–4, no less than eight substantial excavations took place within the central core.

This effort stretched the Lincoln Archaeological Trust beyond its logistic capabilities, and outsiders were called in on two major sites. John Wacher of the University of Leicester sectioned the eastern defences of the lower *colonia* and showed that, in the later second century AD, the extended settlement had been defended by an earth bank topped by a wooden fence. The stone wall of the *colonia* had been a later insertion. In a parallel operation at Saltergate a complete length of the southern defences was uncovered and exposed an unsuspected Roman postern gateway, an internal and external tower close to the gate, and evidence for two stages in the construction of the *colonia* wall. The wall itself produced evidence of modification in the late Saxon or early medieval period, and another part of the site produced organic material from semi-waterlogged layers.

Further excavations at Lincoln added to knowledge of the city's history. While a good deal was understood about the defences and their development in the upper settlement as it grew from legionary fortress to *colonia*, very little was known of the interior. The great majority of the area is given over to the cathedral and castle, and much of the rest is quite rightly designated a conservation area due to the architectural interest of the surviving buildings. As a result, particular interest centred on the redevelopment of the area of St Paul in the Bail. It lay on the presumed site of the headquarters building of the legionary fortress which would have formed the basis for the forum of the later *colonia*.

Rescue excavation by Mick Jones in 1978–9 identified the massive timber post-holes forming part of the cross-hall of the headquarters which could be reconstructed as approximately 65 by 60 metres with an eastward-facing plan. When the site had developed as a civilian centre in the last decade of the first century AD, the headquarters area had continued to serve as a major building unit. Despite the surviving traces of fine paving and even of statue plinths, the plan could not be adequately reconstructed at this stage: much had been swept away by the major redevelopment of the site in the second quarter of the second century under the emperor Hadrian. This was a time when several major building initiatives, such as the construction of the Wroxeter forum, were under way in Roman Britain. The Hadrianic remodelling had involved turning the new forum and basilica through a right angle on to a north-south alignment. The plan, which can now be seen to have included the remarkable upstanding (eight-metres high) Roman structure known as the Mint Wall, incorporates a conventional forum and basilica with a linked temple area that is reminiscent of Continental examples rather than of any elsewhere in Roman Britain.

Yet perhaps the most important discovery at St Paul in the Bail in historical terms belongs to the post-Roman period. Bede's *Ecclesiastical History* informs us that in AD 628–9 Paulinus of York came to Lincoln and built a church. In the headquarters/forum complex the remains of several church plans did indeed emerge from the excavation of the post-Roman levels. The earliest in the sequence was devoid of informative dating material until the discovery of a bronze hanging-bowl found tucked in the corner of a robbed out grave. This distinctive piece of metalwork with enamelled attachments, probably datable to the seventh century, made the earliest church on the site an obvious candidate for the building founded by Paulinus. The history of the subsequent development of the church site reflects the later story of Lincoln. The early church was replaced in the tenth century by another, probably built under the impetus of Danish settlement in the shell of the upper city. Downhill, especially towards the riverside harbour, lay the centres of trade, and it was between the two that the area of Flaxengate developed as a production and marketing centre in the two centuries prior to the Norman conquest.

The lessons of Lincoln are obvious in retrospect. A great historic centre, it had in the post-War years undergone relatively little major change in its central core. Accordingly, archaeological investigation, although in itself important, progressed in the background, and often not in a rescue context, until the 1970s. Then the great redevelopment programme threw archaeology to the fore. The programme meant that archaeological resources were predictably stretched to their limit, and it could be argued that the local authority tried to have its excavation on the cheap. The earlier excavations at the Park and the police headquarters site were disproportionately funded by the Department of the Environment.

When the city authorities eventually did begin funding archaeology, and the director of excavations was appointed, instead of attracting a person of experience, the salary offered was comparable with that of a typist. Inevitably this created conflicts of interest in which the legitimate claims of archaeology were stifled within the local government hierarchy. The picture improved somewhat with the creation of an independent archaeological trust that expanded the existing directorial personnel, even though the creation of the trust occurred at the very time when the politics of Lincoln were at their most acerbic—there were two rival civic societies, and later two rival Labour factions struggling for control of the Labour-dominated city, the whole situation further confounded by local government reorganisation in April 1974. And at least one member of the trust's managing committee wore several hats through involvement in the development schemes around the lower town.

In short, it is fortunate that so much actual excavation was achieved in Lincoln, particularly as financial stringencies soon began to intervene again. As the pressure of redevelopment eases the major task of publication becomes pressing.

Colchester

In the city of Colchester the role of archaeology has undergone a very similar evolution to that of Lincoln. Colchester was the early capital of Roman Britain prior to the Boudiccan revolt in AD 60. It is a site where, until the 1970s, excavational emphasis was placed almost exclusively on the Roman period, a time when the centrepiece of the town was a temple to the deified emperor Claudius, the substructure of which is incorporated in the present castle.

In the 1960s, excavation facilities were an extension of the museum's service, but, with the redevelopment cycle that began in 1970, it was clear that they would be greatly overstretched. The cycle saw the redevelopment of various major sites along the High Street and in the Lion Walk area to the south. The archaeological implications were fortunately recognised with the creation of an independent Colchester Archaeological Unit under the direction of Philip Crummy. As long ago as the 1930s, major excavation had taken place on the immediately pre-Roman tribal centre outside the city, near the Sheepen Dyke, but knowledge of the interior of the present walled area within the city, particularly in the medieval period, was far less advanced. The work of the new archaeological unit went a long way towards rectifying the situation.

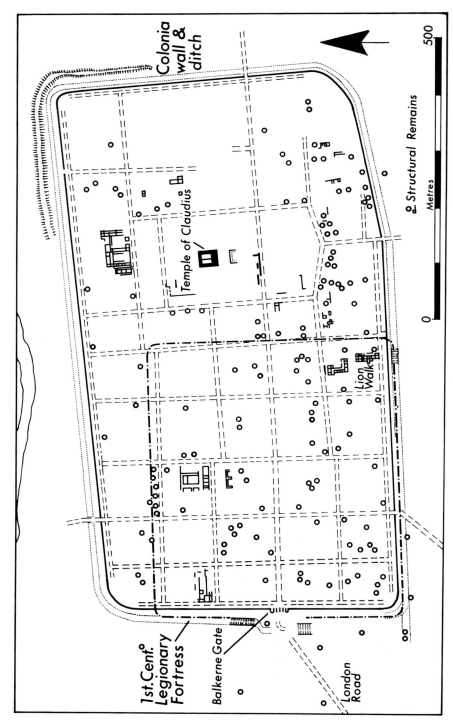

Fig. 27 Roman Colchester. Diagrammatic plan showing the outline of the legionary fortress within the walled area of the Roman colony

From the prolonged excavations in the Lion Walk area, it is now reasonably certain that Colchester began life, as has long been surmised, as a legionary fortress underlying what is now the western portion of the walled town. The occurrence of an inscription relating to the Twentieth Legion, and pre-dating the Boudiccan rebellion, as well as the distribution of Claudian coinage, had already suggested that the first legionary base to be established after the Roman invasion of AD 43 lay somewhere in this area. The Lion Walk excavations located part of the barracks and centurions' blocks belonging to the south-eastern corner of the postulated fortress. The discovery of the eastern ramparts explained the divergences between the road systems in the two halves of the later walled area. The early buildings discovered at Lion Walk showed clear evidence of having been destroyed by the Boudiccan revolt of AD 60, by which time the early fortress was already functioning as a *colonia* inhabited by veterans. The *colonia* was not, therefore, a new foundation, but simply a revitalised legionary fortress. What made the settlement remarkable was the extensive area to the east that contained the temple of Claudius, and, if the Roman historian Tacitus is to be believed, a theatre as well. Although the lack of adequate defences made the colony easy meat for the Boudiccan rebels, pride demanded that the complex be restored once the revolt was quelled. Traces of structures within the *colonia* emerged sporadically during redevelopment in the 1970s, often under salvage conditions, and sometimes denied any kind of ar-chaeological examination—for example, massive walls and foundations over two metres deep were seen in 1969 and 1970 when Cater's and Sainsbury's were redeveloped, but regretfully nothing was done. These remains may well have belonged to a basilica set at one end of the imperial temple complex along similar lines to the layout of the colony at Augst on the Swiss border.

During the 1970s, however, archaeology was far better geared towards meeting the new redevelopment problem. Not least amongst the achievements was the long-awaited confirmation of the medieval potential of the town: Saxon huts were discovered on the Lion Walk site. By the late Saxon period settlement had probably concentrated along the High Street frontage to give the old walled core of the town roughly the same layout as it still retains. After a brief occupation by the Danes in the early tenth century, the invaders were driven out by Edward the Elder, son of Alfred the Great, who apparently turned Colchester into a strongpoint against Danish incursions; Sir Mortimer Wheeler suggested that the Balkerne Gate, the western entrance to the city, had been blocked at this stage. Evidence of a ditch possibly datable to this period was also recovered in the area of Vineyard Street, and may have formed part of a complete defensive circuit.

The principal stone buildings of the late Saxon period were the churches, often deriving their structural materials directly from Roman remains, as did the Romanesque campanile of Colchester's Holy Trinity. From the Norman period the excavations also uncovered domestic structures, principally a house from the Lion Walk area which had survived in a remarkably well-preserved condition, perhaps because of substantial modification and rebuilding in about the sixteenth century. By this time, and indeed probably for centuries earlier, the street system of the town centre had crystallised into roughly the form in which it survives today, and practically all visible remains of the Roman town, with the exception of the gates and walls, had disappeared from view.

The almost continuous process of excavation in Colchester after 1970 was triggered off by the redevelopment programme within the walled area. Outside this, the creation of an inner relief road opened up the possibility of examining the extensive cemeteries around the town, and the new northern bypass also produced valuable information about Bronze Age cemeteries and settlement in the Chitts Hill area west of the Belgic capital that was the forerunner of Colchester itself. Aerial photography of this area, like that of the pre-Roman tribal capital around Gosbecks to the south of the city, made it clear that, from the wealth of crop marks evident every year, all development, particularly gravel-quarrying, needed to be carefully examined for its archaeological implications so that excavation could take place in advance. Most of the threats of the 1970s were met by increased finances and by new cooperation between archaeologists and the city council which allowed the vital Lion Walk excavation to take place between demolition and redevelopment.

Gloucester

The situation at Colchester found close parallels with that at Gloucester. Until the 1970s, the latter city generally had an image based on its role as a great cathedral town with a wealth of medieval and post-medieval buildings. But this was not long to be the case. The centre of Gloucester was probably modernised faster than any other city in the country. In approximately the three decades since the War something like 150 historic buildings were removed, and the scale of redevelopment that this implies should have led to co-ordination with rescue archaeology much sooner than it did. Unhappily, in the event, when Henry Hurst was appointed as City Archaeologist in 1968, much of the redevelopment had already taken place, and throughout his office he was left to excavate Gloucester with only a subvention from the city authorities that in the early years amounted to no more than £250 annually.

The task that he had to face was a very complicated one in interpretative terms. The line of Ermine Street, the principal Roman

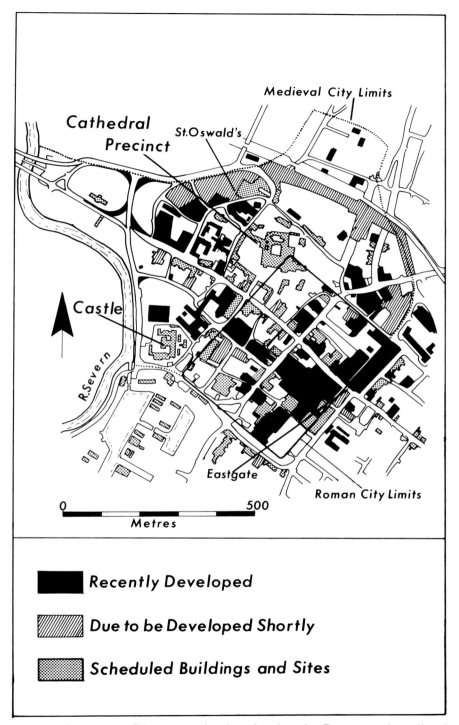

Medieval City Limits

Cathedral
Precinct

St.Oswald's

Castle

R.Severn

Eastgate

Roman City Limits

0 ————— 500
Metres

▇▇ Recently Developed

▨▨ Due to be Developed Shortly

▨▨ Scheduled Buildings and Sites

Fig. 28 Gloucester. Diagrammatic plan showing the Roman and medieval walled towns

89

Fig. 29 Gloucester. A rescue excavation site in the legionary fortress area

road of the area, leads not directly to Gloucester but to the modern suburb of Kingsholm, and it was there that quantities of military equipment were uncovered during house construction in the first half of this century. Not unreasonably this discovery led to the theory that the base to which the Twentieth Legion was probably transferred in AD 49 from Colchester lay in this northern suburb. The evidence had to be assimilated with the fact that a colony was created at Gloucester in the final years of the first century AD. The obvious site for the *colonia* was the walled area of the modern city approaching some 60 acres in size. But this neat theory suffered a rough blow in 1959–60, when the late Sir Ian

Richmond sectioned the city defences of Gloucester and produced, from the earliest phase, the remains of a legionary oven set in the back of a normal military-style rampart and ditch. There matters rested for a decade until the wave of rescue work in the early years of the 1970s corroborated Richmond's interpretation.

Excavation took place in four main areas, spread out in a strip across the centre of the city. On the east, a large area of the new Woolworth's basement was excavated and revealed traces of military barracks alongside the central headquarters range. In the centre of the town examination on the redeveloped site of the old Bell Hotel disclosed part of a forum complex, presumably overlying the earlier legionary headquarters building. To the west, the telephone exchange site produced detailed evidence of the development of barrack blocks into the structures of the *colonia* period. The foundation of the military phase dates to some time after AD 60, so the old theory was proved correct in identifying Kingsholm as a military site, although of only limited time-span. It became clear during excavation that the legionary barracks had not been abandoned, but rather were continuously occupied into the *colonia* phase. The first colonists, who were in any case presumably legionary veterans, had lived on in the pre-existing legionary barracks, a situation similar to that described in several passages of Tacitus, writing of Italy in the Julio-Claudian period. Gloucester provided the first archaeological evidence in Europe for development of this kind.

The Roman walled area provided the basis for the medieval development of the wall circuit northwards and westwards to enclose areas closer to the River Severn, and by the end of Henry I's reign, there was in effect a continuous line of defence from the eastern side of the old *colonia* to the river. On the southern side this line comprised the southern Roman wall and the castle defences, on the northern, part of the Roman wall and the precinct walls of St Peter's Abbey and St Oswald's Priory. At this time the river and the marshy area to the west had probably provided sufficient defence. This state of affairs appears to have ended in the mid-thirteenth century with the development of Westgate bridge, probably as part of a major refortification that further extended the size of the medieval town.

A sample of the internal buildings was examined in Northgate Street when a timber-framed building was demolished under controlled conditions and subsequently excavated. Like Colchester, Gloucester is richly endowed with documentary sources for the early medieval period. The material derives from the connection with cathedral landholdings and from the registers of Llanthony Priory on the edge of the city. The use of documents helps to refine the objectives of rescue work. A Rental of the Northgate Street area of 1455 refers to a 'tenement . . . wherein John Tanner holdsand exercised his calling'. The area had constituted a commercial quarter from its foundation and served successively as a tannery, as implied by the document, a public house, a cooked meat purveyors, and ultimately, a barber's shop.

From the mid-1970s archaeology in Gloucester underwent a second evolution. Emphasis moved away from desperate rescue or salvage operations to planned excavations in advance of development in a context where an increasing amount of the documentary and historical background was known. In the initial phase, archaeology came to Gloucester too late. This is reflected in the budget: total expenditure on archaeology for 1971–2 and 1972–3, was £2,433 and £3,332 respectively—and these figures included the salary of the field officer. But in 1973 there were dramatic changes: the budget available rose to £15,000 and a museum excavation unit was created, jointly financed by the Department of the Environment and Gloucester Corporation. In 1976, the new unit, under its second director, Carolyn Heighway, began tackling such problems as the redevelopment of the East Gate site in the city centre where the Roman gateway underwent considerable modification in medieval times, and indeed in the early modern period when it was refurbished to face attack in the Civil War.

Exeter

The walled town of Exeter has always played an important historical role in the development of the South West. It was bomb damage in the heart of the shopping area that enabled Lady Fox to carry out limited rescue excavation work in the city centre as long ago as 1945. Flimsy timber buildings of Roman date were found, but the results were on too limited a scale to allow major deductions about the nature of the occupation. For the next 20 years genteel scholastic disagreement ignored the manifest problems of Exeter's medieval archaeological potential and centred on the nature of occupation in the Roman period: was the site always a civilian one, evolving into the walled cantonal capital that forms the historic defences of the city today? Or did the city follow the more normal pattern with a military occupation preceding civilian growth? In the event the answer was as unexpected as it was impressive.

In the last years of the 1960s, John Collis, a lecturer at the University of Exeter, began a series of excavations on sloping ground in the Guildhall area of the city. He located a series of elongated timber buildings with detached rectangular structures at their ends which resembled nothing less than military barracks and separate centurions' quarters. These implications were viewed somewhat sceptically at the time, but spectacular excavational results in the 1970s confirmed the evidence of Collis's work.

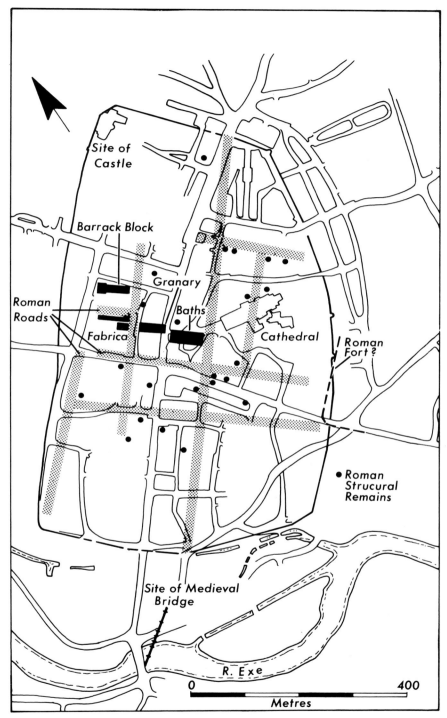

Fig. 30 Exeter. Diagrammatic plan showing the principal archaeological discoveries of the 1960s and 1970s

Site of Castle

Barrack Block

Granary

Roman Roads

Baths

Fabrica

Cathedral

Roman Fort?

● Roman Strucural Remains

Site of Medieval Bridge

R. Exe

0   400

Metres

Fig. 31　Excavations in Cathedral Close, Exeter 1972

By 1971 an archaeological excavation unit had been established in
the city under the direction of Michael Griffiths. The formation of such
a team was in line with developments in others of the more far-sighted
historic centres. While the archaeological unit was continuing work in
the Guildhall area, an opportunity arose for a major excavation on the
site of the church of St Mary Major fronting the west door of the
cathedral. In the initial phase discoveries of the Roman period
comprised a massive bath-house, with a vast *caldarium* or hot room. The
principal plunge baths lay at either end of the short axis, while two semi-
circular recesses along the southern side contained the foundations for
two enormous *labra*, or basins, of Purbeck marble. The internal tiled
jacketing associated with the hypocaust arrangements was of a type
which went out of fashion in Italy around the middle of the first century
AD. Indeed, it is precisely to this period that the origins of the building
relate: construction of the bath is dated between AD 55 and 60.

The area to the north around the Guildhall with its traces of barracks,
a workshop and a granary, taken in conjunction with the bath-house,
covers an area large enough to suggest the presence of a legionary
fortress underlying this part of the 92-acre walled city. The very size and
date of the baths would point in that direction in any case. Thus it is
here that the second Augustan Legion must have been based in the years
following the initial difficult conquest of the south-western tribes,
especially the Durotriges of Dorset. Quite where the defensive circuit for
a 50- to 60-acre military site runs, however, was not discovered.

94

If the earliest phase of the baths underlying St Mary Major proved to offer such important evidence, so, too, did the details of their alteration for the development of the structure into the civilian phase. Around AD 75 the baths were modified by the removal of hypocausts from the former *tepidarium* and by the division of the main hot room into two. This change was the prelude to a major rearrangement of the structure around AD 90: the baths were converted into a *basilica* or large hall, probably forming part of the forum complex that is evidence of the transition from military to civilian control and of the establishment at Exeter of the cantonal capital of the Dumnonii of Devon and Cornwall. The *basilica* underwent further alteration with the insertion of an elongated room in the south-eastern corner, perhaps used by officials for the less important everyday proceedings. The south-eastern corner was again the focus of remodelling in the late fourth century, and possibly later. (The difficulty in establishing a precise chronology is a result of the insertion of Saxon graves throughout much of this area.) A number of hypotheses can be adduced that might establish a relationship between the development of the Roman bath building into the religious forerunner of St Mary Major, and ultimately of the cathedral itself after Bishop Leofric established his seat at Exeter in 1050.

The results of work by the unit under Griffiths cast a revolutionary light on previous assumptions about Exeter. The presence of a legionary fortress, and also, at some other stage in the mid-first century, of a substantial fort to the south, are today taken as established. But there is also increasing evidence concerning the medieval period. Despite the lack of precisely dated ceramic evidence to corroborate historical supposition, there is considerable reason to believe that the town survived well into the fifth century, and indeed probably survived in recognisable form until the Saxon period. From written history it is known that Exeter was a major centre in the Saxon period, on a par with London, Winchester and York: such was its importance that the inhabitants felt strong enough to challenge William the Conqueror. If, as was probably the case, the bulk of the Saxon city of Exeter was concentrated along the four principal streets, then over half of the possible archaeological evidence has already been destroyed.

Yet, despite such loss, Exeter's great advantage has been that full provision for the archaeological element in redevelopment programmes, and not simply the creation of a rescue excavation unit, was carefully and deliberately created during the 1970s. The city was as far ahead as any in its approach to the conflict between the past and the present. Indeed, in the second half of the decade its local authority was probably well in advance of most others in that it not only had a declared and accepted policy to deal with archaeological problems, but it also put its money where its mouth was. From 1972–4 local authority expenditure on rescue archaeology rose from £14,000 to nearly £21,000, which was substantially more than contributions from the Department of the Environment. Moreover, in October 1974 the full council accepted a policy document emanating from the management team (that is, all chief officers, including those in the planning and treasurer's sections), which established the field archaeology unit as a permanent section of the authority, thereby accepting any financial implications. This move was aimed to cover all the potential fields of activity that were in fact subsequently developed. Rescue archaeology was no longer treated as a small part of a major problem, but was subsumed into environmental policy as a whole, and the field unit became involved in working parties covering projects such as land use, planning, transportation and conservation.

The basis for such a fruitful co-operation between theoretically conflicting interests goes back to the Civil Amenities Act (1967) as it related to Exeter. This had given the city planners the opportunity to incorporate archaeological considerations into questions of planning permission. Thus, archaeological examination was built into the programme affecting all sites where the local authority was the redeveloper. In 1974 a clause allowing for archaeology was also included where necessary in private planning permissions to the effect that 'adequate provision be made for archaeological investigation of the site.'

As the policy document of October 1974 had emphasised, 'no legislation exists to make it necessary to carry out adequate investigation of archaeologically sensitive areas threatened by development. Nonetheless, the council considered it necessary to implement such a policy in view of the undoubted importance of the historic city of Exeter.' The council went on to regret, that since 1970 no legal directions or even general guidelines had been given to developers either public or private, in dealing with archaeologically important zones. Such a national problem related directly to the Department of the Environment and to the pressures that its ministers could create to secure parliamentary time for any proposed legislation dealing with this problem. After existing in draft for several years, it was only in April 1979 that the Ancient Monuments and Archaeological Areas Act was at last passed.

7
Moveable Feasts: Wales

The Welsh branch of the Inspectorate of the Department of the Environment has always appeared liberal in its interpretation of the Department's guidelines. It was the first to declare that the annual ploughing of a site constituted a rescue threat, and thus made the decision to finance total excavation of the Whitton villa in the Glamorgan plain in the 1960s. The dwarf stone walls of the later farm structures of the villa lay only centimetres below ground-level and every season's ploughing brought the tell-tale litter of building stone and pottery to the surface, like the flotsam from a submerged wreck. The site was of particular importance, as the excavations by Michael Jarrett, showed. He traced its development from a series of concentric late Iron Age huts set within a ditched compound, to the rectangular buildings of the mid-Roman period. The excavation led to an understanding of the way in which ancient farms developed under the impact of Romanisation in the Vale of Glamorgan.

The principle of plough damage was also the reason for the complete excavation in 1970 of Walesland Rath, further west in Pembrokeshire, by one of the Department's own inspectors, Geoffrey Wainwright. With unusually substantial funding he was able to complete a thorough area-stripping of the interior and of parts of the defences. The results were impressive, revealing the internal details of another late Iron Age structure, but one that had not 'developed' to the stage of having stone-built Roman-period buildings. The two excavations taken together revolutionised knowledge of this kind of late Iron Age/Roman rural site in South Wales, and constituted one of the earliest examples of the far-sighted recognition of rescue threats and action upon them by a national body.

The Welsh Inspectorate also went further in other directions in pioneering generous use of supporting funds for full and prompt publication. But perhaps its most notable contribution to rescue archaeology was one particularly attuned to the less numerous yet dispersed rescue threats within the principality: in 1970 a mobile excavation team—Rescue Archaeology Group (RAG)—was formed, the members of which were to be distributed on a series of projects as need arose. The scheme was fostered by the Chief Inspector of the time, Dr Michael Apted, and his lieutenant, David Morgan-Evans. For its implementation, however, it depended on the enterprise of Chris Musson, a mature student in the Department of Archaeology at University College, Cardiff. An architect by training, he saw an opportunity for applying the concept of architectural group practice in the context of Welsh archaeology.

A small team of highly trained personnel were to tackle a series of projects for which the members would be personally responsible from the pre-planning and excavation stages to final publication. As one project director moved from excavation to begin the process of publication, the supporting members would be re-allocated to other projects. They would operate all the year round, irrespective of weather conditions, and were to be paid at considerably more than the subsistence rates normally offered to volunteers on rescue excavations. In 1970 rates were £1.75 per day for volunteers living away from home, and clearly such rates would have been impossibly inadequate for the maintenance of a team on a year-round basis.

Under Chris Musson and Graeme Guilbert, from 1970 until 1975 RAG continuously carried out survey work and excavation on Welsh archaeological sites—prehistoric, Roman and medieval—which were threatened with destruction. The text of the group's original 1970 prospectus goes some way towards explaining the success of a small group of this kind.

> The Group works on an entirely professional basis, with a small team of 6–8 excavators, plus a 'back-up' staff to deal with finds and administration. No 'volunteers' are employed, and each member of the Group is expected to carry out the full range of excavation tasks, from turf-stripping and heavy picking to final recording of excavation results. Team-members must therefore possess a good range of skills in surveying, photography and recording in addition to more than usual ability and speed in the standard tasks of excavation and interpretation. They must be fit, strong, willing to work long hours in all sorts of weather, and able to cope with fairly frequent moves from one part of the country to another. They must be able to supervise and interpret their own work, and to take part actively in group-discussions and policy-formulation. Above all they must be sympathetic to the idea of working co-operatively within a small group of near-equals, rather than individually within a group composed of 'leaders' and 'led'. . . .
>
> New members of the Group will have the satisfaction of participating in rescue excavation at the very highest level of professional competence, and in developing new and refined techniques of excavation, recording and interpretation. . . .

Musson's scheme could not have worked, however, without a guaranteed succession of sites, and, in this respect, he was doubly fortunate in the attitude of the Welsh Inspectorate. Because of the country's size, the total number of potential rescue excavations in Wales has always naturally been less than in England, but more predictable thanks to the limited urbanisation. And the aim of RAG, as expressed by David Morgan-Evans, an Inspector at the time, was to eliminate salvage work altogether and, through careful planning, ensure that each potential rescue operation would receive the advantages of time and adequate finance in order to give it the status of a research project.

The very existence of the RAG team or, as cynics preferred to put it, Parkinson's Law, therefore guaranteed its own continuous programme. In the relatively small area of Wales, the RAG scheme meant the avoidance of major overheads when establishing excavations in one part of the country after another. Some of the work—and RAG once operated in England as well—was related purely to one site; later it was co-ordinated within area rescue programmes as the Inspectorate developed larger-scale schemes in advance of other projects, for example, the Brenig dam in 1972–4.

The first major excavation by RAG was at the site of the hill-fort of the Breiddin, the towering limestone mass overlooking the northernmost bend of the Severn, north of Welshpool. The rescue context was the quarrying on the mountainside. Despite frost and snow Musson's team gradually realised that there were considerable technical advantages in their year-round method of operation. In a relatively brief summer excavation period, the prevalence of fast-drying conditions can often make it very difficult to detect the marginal changes in soil texture and coloration on which the archaeological reconstruction of timber buildings so much depends. In the more static conditions of autumn, winter and spring, the RAG team were able to produce significantly more evidence of post-holes and timber partitions than even larger excavation teams would have been able to when operating during brief periods in the summer months.

With a small team and few absolute restrictions on time RAG was able to experiment with a variety of new approaches, including the large-scale exposure of defences such as at Llanstephan and at the north gate of the Roman fort at Caernarvon. But probably at no place was the value of this area-stripping better shown than in the rescue excavation of the site of a small reservoir within the Flintshire hill-fort of Moel-y-Gaer, an excavation that was of dual importance—in terms of both finance and results—in the development of hill-fort archaeology in the 1970s.

The site occupies a detached, rounded hill at the south-eastern end of the mining area of Halkyn Mountain, the whale-backed limestone ridge that runs parallel to the Dee estuary. In 1972 the Inspectorate secured a 50 per cent contribution to the costs of excavation from the developers,

Fig. 32   Excavations at Moel-y-Gaer, Clwyd

the Flintshire Water Board, placing the site in a unique and favoured position in Britain, and akin to that in Scandinavia. There, the developer is legally compelled to make a substantial contribution to the prior examination of development sites, if there is a suggestion of archaeological potential. Moel-y-Gaer proved an all too isolated example of this principle being applied in Britain in the 1970s.

As a result of the exceptional funding, a substantial rampart area could be stripped and, in turn, showed far more of its history than the narrower, more conventional section would have done. The aerial photograph (Fig. 32) shows the line of the palisade of stakes that formed the first defence around the site, probably in the late Bronze Age.

A palisade, common in the original phase of many of the Scottish Border settlements, was also a feature of the later defences at Moel-y-Gaer, but in this case as the final crest of a massive rampart. Careful excavation of a third of the hilltop by Graeme Guilbert with a section of the RAG team in 1973–5, revealed (apart from the foundations of a beacon of the Napoleonic War period!) the four- and six-post arrangements that indicated the internal layout of rectangular houses in the Iron Age.

In the 1970s such houses, termed 'four-posters' or 'six-posters' by archaeologists, were still thought to have been highly uncommon on a hill-fort site in Wales. Circular huts with little or no sign of general planned layout were thought to be the rule despite Stanley Stanford's excavation of a small area within the hill-fort of Credenhill on the Herefordshire border at the end of the 1960s. This had produced unequivocal evidence of four-post house construction and, even though Professor Barry Cunliffe's work within the Danebury hill-fort in Hampshire from 1975 demonstrated that four-posters and six-posters were the rule rather than the exception, it took the Moel-y-Gaer excavations to confirm this new-found pattern and to extend it to the Highland Zone.

How successful was the Rescue Archaeology Group? It was not conceived of as a flying squad to be called out at a moment's notice, but as a professional organisation with an established programme of excavations, arranged preferably a year in advance. RAG thus brought a major element of research to rescue archaeology in Wales. In 1975 the group effectively became the archaeological unit with responsibility for Clwyd and Powys, so that job security was provided for the bulk of the team, and the first founders of the group were proved justified in their committal to the idea of rescue excavation on a full-time professional basis. The ultimate success of their projects will only be judged when they are finally published.

But what of the underlying assumptions of high productivity and standards? A trained specialist group member could obviously achieve a far greater productivity than the relatively less-skilled volunteer, and Chris Musson had claimed that one good professional could do as much work as three volunteers, and should, therefore, be paid three times their wages. Although completely objective comparisons of productivity and cost effectiveness are impossible, Musson's comparison between a winter season on the Breiddin hill-fort and the volunteer-based summer seasons on the hill-fort of South Cadbury (where Musson was himself supervisor) revealed that, in terms of cost, there was little or no difference overall between the two operations.

In the small professional group, the work was faster, and administration and supervision absorbed a minimal amount of time, although the skilled personnel operated on above-average pay. Thus, where the complexity of the task was comparable at both sites, as in the excavation of rampart sections of South Cadbury and at the Breiddin, the cost, relative to size, was comparable: RAG's standard of excavation overall was higher and the ability of the individuals to record and interpret, in particular, was greater, so that, in the long term, the work was completed to a faster programme. For work in the interiors, however, the small group proved more expensive to operate, largely because of greater complexities in the subsoil. But the rock-strewn interior of the Breiddin made it highly unsuitable for the deployment of a large excavation force in any case, and the technicalities of excavation were such that they were most efficiently dealt with by the small highly skilled group. Contemporary excavation of the Roman fortress at Usk could, on the other hand, successfully proceed with a larger team.

With the RAG team the Welsh Inspectorate was able to tackle some of the dispersed rescue problems of Wales. Indeed, the group participated in one of the most intensive operations ever mounted in Wales, the excavations in the Brenig Valley in advance of flooding from dam construction. The task, which involved one of the richer groups of prehistoric sites from the uplands of North Wales, was a three-year project, carefully planned so that it would be a real opportunity for research. After a preliminary season of field survey in 1972, primarily designed to establish the extent of cairnfields, the main programme of excavations took place in 1973. The scale of the operation demanded multiple direction. Apart from the involvement of RAG, directors came from University College, Bangor, and the Universities of Manchester and Galway. Eighty to 100 diggers had to work at over 1,000 feet. The work encompassed a variety of monuments ranging from barrows and ring cairns (one dated by radio-carbon to between 1680 ± 100 BC and 1280 ± 70 BC) to a post-medieval settlement.

Several prehistoric barrows were totally excavated by Frances Lynch of Bangor giving insight not only into the details of their construction but also into the prevailing environment in the Bronze Age through soil and pollen samples taken from the land surface sealed beneath the barrows. And work by Chris Musson's group in 1974 extended to examining a medieval *hafod*, or steading, perched on the moorland overlooking the barrows. The programme was conducted on a sufficiently large scale to give the varied mass of information recovered an overall research perspective. Together it showed how the upland landscape had developed across four millenia. A second digging season in 1974 was on a lesser scale and related to sites destined to be submerged by the second-stage water level of the reservoir.

Altogether, with adequate forward planning and a budget that exceeded the normal annual expenditure on rescue work in the whole of Scotland at the time, the Brenig project showed that, at their best, the distinction between rescue archaeology and research becomes meaningless. The lessons from Brenig were subsequently applied in a similar situation created by extensions to the Elan Valley reservoirs.

When Wales benefited from increased funding made available in the mid-1970s, the organisational solution adopted in the light of such operations as that at Brenig proved to be one of the better decisions of its kind. Within it, broadly speaking, geographic and academic considerations were harmonised: in 1975 the division of the principality into four areas—Dyfed in the south-west, Gwynedd in the north-west, Clwyd and Powys east and north-east (where the core of Chris Musson's team was reconstituted) and Glamorgan and Gwent in the south-east—gave each area its own archaeological unit operating under the umbrella of a trust. The units have since made a substantial contribution to archaeological knowledge with a series of excavations or surveys at Caernarvon, Aberffraw, Dinorben, Flint, Carmarthen, Swansea, Cowbridge and Caerleon.

Wales can be described as the area where an advanced methodology was evolved to meet the needs of rural rescue archaeology, but there was not commensurate progress on the urban side. To a considerable extent this stemmed from the lack of major redevelopment in the historic town centres. For instance, in the *Erosion of History* the town of Ruthin was chosen for study and it became apparent that little of archaeological importance was liable to be disturbed during the 1970s; the bomb-shattered centre of Swansea was rebuilt long before the rescue archaeology movement; the programme of work on medieval Cardiff by Peter Webster, extra-mural tutor in Archaeology at University College, Cardiff, was limited outside the castle by the lack of available sites; and changes in towns like Pembroke lay outside the historic core. A certain amount of work was possible in the early 1970s within the walled areas of Conway and also at Abergavenny, where traces of an early fort from the period of the Roman invasion were located. The Welsh Inspectorate initiated important programmes of excavation south of the Edwardian medieval castle of Rhuddlan and on the major Roman invasion base on the south side of Usk. In the latter two cases the work was conducted largely on open sites prior to building operations extending the modern built-up area.

The excavations at Carmarthen from 1968 to 1972 by the author were thus a rare example of larger-scale urban archaeology in Wales. The work there was a first attempt to examine the last major Roman settlement in Wales, and the programme of excavations was an example of an individual archaeologist incorporating rescue excavation within an overall research programme. Excavation took place to a tight time-schedule, both within the nucleus of the modern town and on wider-spread redevelopment sites that proved to lie within the area of the Roman walled settlement. The work presented many difficulties, not least of which was the opposition of the local museum that had effectively blocked major initiative in this area for a quarter of a century! As a result the excavation programme required the presence of a colleague whose principal task lay in securing permission for excavation to be carried out at all: the co-operation of the Urban District Council was essential if excavation was to be on a sufficiently large scale. If the work at Carmarthen had a value other than archaeological, it lay in showing the kind of processes involved in securing an effective archaeological presence in a town where none had existed previously (see Table 4).

The season in 1968 marked the first stage of the programme. The probable area of Flavian military occupation was located, as was the outline of the wall circuit associated with the Roman cantonal capital, and, as an unexpected bonus, its amphitheatre to the west. In view of the pressures of time and minimal finance, only imported, hand-picked volunteers were used for this part of the operation.

An area outside the town scheduled for redevelopment as the town's major car park had qualified for a rescue grant, and the major season in 1969 examined $1\frac{1}{4}$ acres in detail. This time, to answer the changed requirements, the approach was very different, and local volunteers were deliberately encouraged and integrated with the imported volunteer excavators. Permanent and local contacts were necessary, in addition to the invaluable help of the local builder who had lent equipment from the very start. The most important require-ment was a local agent to co-ordinate the town's developing interest with that of the archaeologists while the excavators were away. He was instrumental in setting up a local appeal fund backed by the Mayor of Carmarthen and the Chairman of the Rural District Council. Public enthusiasm meant that guided tours were offered daily and a special open day towards the end of the excavation brought in the public in their hundreds.

The long-term results of these efforts extended far beyond the immediate excavation. The presence of archaeological activity led to the re-growth of the local archaeological society in 1969 and its swift growth, encouraged by public displays and lectures around the town, to become the largest in Wales. Under this impetus the annual journal reappeared and has subsequently been published regularly; and in the new atmosphere the process of rescue archaeology became readily accepted by local government and public alike and is continued by the Dyfed Archaeological Trust, which under Heather James has continued to excavate the Roman Cantonal capital of the Demetae, as Carmarthen is now recognised to be.

The 1970 season was concerned with excavation within the amphi-theatre. Again, the kind of excavation team was altered in relation to the expected problems: a general lack of finds and the complex task of unravelling the timber supports that underpinned the seating on the north bank of the amphitheatre. After these came the problems of conservation and of the public presentation of the amphitheatre. A redevelopment programme on the south side of the amphitheatre was so adjusted by the co-operative Urban District Council that it became

TABLE 4 Carmarthen project. Development sequence 1967–72

	Public relations	Finance	Archaeology	Spin-off
1967	Publicity relations officer plus director. Prospective mayor, other aldermen and town clerk etc. canvassed. Newspaper campaign			(Local Archaeological Society moribund; no journal for 6 years)
	Urban District Council permits small excavation	Board of Celtic Studies: £250	*Excavation* *Phase I: Preliminary* Basic location of fort	Help from local businessmen. Agitation in Archaeological Society leads to take-over by active members
1968	Full newspaper coverage. Main local agent selected		Outline of cantonal capital and amphitheatre	Archaeological Society reconstituted. Journal printed with 1968 interim report. Some conservation by Urban District Council
1969	Joint Rural District Council/County Council appeal. On-site guides, displays etc. Public open days and lectures	Ministry of Public Building and Works etc.: c. £2,100 Local appeal: £400 Total: c. £2,500	*Phase II: Major season* 4 weeks. 60–80 volunteers including local volunteers. Volunteers including local volunteers	Urban District Council decision to conserve amphitheatre as monument
1970	Publicity dropped until final stages	Board of Celtic Studies: £250	*Phase III: Amphitheatre* Small, selected excavation team	Journal printed with 1969 interim report. New society membership reaches 450
1971	Re-application of publicity to secure land access	Board of Celtic Studies: etc.: £270 +	*Field survey* of settlement sites in countryside. Trial excavation of late Iron Age/Roman site/s to assess programme	Start made with air photographic survey. New museum director appointed. Society participates
1972			*Excavation of agricultural site on large scale*	Interim presentation of field work results in journal 1973. Society takes major part

possible to turf and display the bulk of the amphitheatre area (see Fig. 33). Progress of this kind was much facilitated since a member of the original digging team of 1969 had become curator of the local museum, and it was under his aegis that the enthusiasm for rescue archaeology was extended to work in the surrounding countryside.

In 1972, the new curator, John Little, intent on examining the history of native agricultural sites in the area, completed a survey of known archaeological potential within the whole of the county. This survey was promptly incorporated into the programme of the County Planning Office, so that Carmarthenshire was one of the two counties in Wales (the other is Anglesey) where archaeological factors are guaranteed integration within the early phases of the planning process.

It is indeed in the planning area that the most important advances were made in Wales in the 1970s. If there were not many obvious and immediate urban threats in the 1960s, it was because re-development in the smaller historic towns like Montgomery, Denbigh, Llanidloes, Builth Wells and Brecon was slow and archaeological potential unknown. Archaeological potential can only be assessed from historical and documentary sources, and, in Wales in 1974 an initiative by the Department of the Environment allotted an historical researcher to the Archaeology Department of University College, Cardiff.

This welcome move was also paralleled in the legislative field in the case of Dolaucothi mines. The Roman and post-Roman mining site at

Fig. 33 The landscaped Roman amphitheatre, Carmarthen, after excavation in 1970

Dolaucothi in south-west Wales represents the most technologically advanced example of ancient mining in Britain. Since 1971 there had been pressure for its preservation *in toto* as an area of special historical (as well as geological and ecological) interest, a policy actively pursued by the National Trust who own much of the site. The mines had already suffered considerable destruction from afforestation and deep ploughing with caterpillar tractors on marginal land, and only block-scheduling of large areas could have conserved what was left of the mining zones and the hydraulic features associated with them in the Roman period. Such a scheme at that time did not normally find official favour, but it is to the Welsh Inspectorate's credit, and consistent with the attitude revealed throughout the 1970s—in many ways exemplary in comparison with attitudes in England and Scotland—that it was implemented.

The most important move, however, as already indicated, was the re-organisation of rescue archaeology along new lines in the latter part of the decade. The Principality was entrusted to four Trusts, one of which was composed of members of the RAG and based on Clwyd–Powys. The second Trust covered Glamorgan–Gwent, while the Gwynedd and Dyfed Trusts catered for the north-west and south-west respectively. The four Trusts have divided the financial cake supplied by the Welsh branch of the Department of Environment relatively amicably with the annual division reflecting the particular priorities of the given year. On the whole the arrangement worked well in the geographically logical areas, though from the beginning the Clwyd–Powys team faced a nonsensically elongated area with stretched communications (but one fortunately underpinned by the presence of John Manley as archaeological officer for Clwyd proper).

The results have been impressive overall. The Gwynedd Trust initially carried out important excavations at Caernarvon and more recently examined in great detail a long-lived native settlement at Cefn Graeanog between Caernarvon and Portmadoc. The Clwyd–Powys Trust, already involved in work at the Breiddin, moved on to excavate two other important hill-forts at Moel-y-Gaer on Deeside and Dinorben near Colwyn Bay. The Dyfed Trust has continued excavations of the Roman Cantonal capital at Carmarthen and begun an important programme on rural sites in Dyfed. The Glamorgan–Gwent Trust, under the direction of Gareth Dowdell, has excavated and surveyed on a very broad scale in its appointed area, and made some notable discoveries principally in the Roman period. These include excavations of the fort at Loughor, the important but still incompletely understood site at Cowbridge and an enigmatic courtyard structure overlooking the Bristol channel at Cold Knap, Barry.

But it is clear that the honeymoon period is now over. For the

Glamorgan–Gwent Trust, disaster came in the most obvious form. On the night of the 13th March 1983, fire destroyed half the Trust's premises, comprising a large warehouse, two offices and a photographic studio and darkroom. Most of the material from 60 sites, including important excavations at Caerleon, Cowbridge, Loughor and Usk, was lost along with plans, find records and photographic archives from the various sites. The underlying question is *why* much of this archive had to be stored in second class premises rather than under better protection in museum storage. The answer is that the necessary storage facilities in museums had not grown to keep pace with rescue archaeology and the Trust, already relying on inadequate core finances, simply could not provide the requisite standard of storage facilities. The real cost of the losses through that disastrous fire have still to be worked out, but are obviously likely to affect the production of final reports in the coming years.

The basic problem confronting all four Welsh Trusts, however, is lack of realistic financing for the foreseeable future. Rescue threats in the current financial climate are likely to appear rapidly as development finance becomes available. The £350,000 made available by the Welsh Office and divided between the four trusts is simply not enough to allow a proper programme related to the actual rescue situation. If we take the Glamorgan-Gwent Trust again as an example, it requires additional money to finance the existing important project at Loughor and its officers are even more concerned at the lack of adequate access and finance for a major project at Cowbridge.

While the Welsh Trusts have these problems, it is always important to retain a sense of scale. In 1973 one excavation in Wales prior to the construction of the Brenig Dam received more finance than the total rescue budget for Scotland. Now in 1983 the latest information from Scotland suggests that, from the overall budget of approximately half a million pounds designed to cover all aspects of archaeological work, a mere £150,000 is earmarked for rescue archaeology on urban sites in Scotland. This figure is approximately the same as the budget for two Welsh Trusts, or more to the point, one substantial scheme initiated by the Manpower Services Commission elsewhere. Despite all the improvements in Scotland, described in the next chapter, the porridge is still very thin.

8

'Part of our Scottish Kindness'

In the early 1970s it was arguable, and with considerable justification, that Scottish archaeology was in a singular state of atrophy despite the academic support of the universities and a distinguished Royal Commission. It was even arguable that the contribution of outsiders, particularly in the Roman field, equalled, if it did not outweigh, that of the home universities.

At that time the Scottish equivalent of the Department of the Environment's Inspectorate—the Property Services Agency—was widely known for, and partly hamstrung by, lack of internal cohesion, and the university departments were divided by fresh appointments and new trends in archaeology. Although the screen of formal unanimity could be re-erected to face informed criticism such as that cogently delivered by Ian Crawford, in the most pithy chapter of *Rescue Archaeology* (1974), the situation took no account of the deep-rooted dissatisfaction of the younger generation of archaeologists or of the divisive image presented by archaeology, particularly in local government. John Knox had taken a 'sober pride' in the national pastime of feuding, or what he termed 'part of our Scottish kindness', and the trend was thought by some to be too deeply entrenched to be changed. Fortunately by 1978 the situation had changed.

At a conference in St Andrews in 1975 the Chief Planning Officer asked a representative of the Scottish Inspectorate the amount of the annual budget for rescue archaeology in Scotland. The reply was £25,000 per annum on average. 'Peanuts—' shouted the Planning Officer, 'Do you know how much Fife receives for tidying up a few miles of road? £125,000.' The local government officials in the conference were amazed at the paucity of central government finance, and testified that the county authority had not once been approached by the Scottish Inspectorate in an attempt to secure local government funds on a parity with, for example, those awarded for Nicholas Brook's work in medieval St Andrews in 1973.

In 1975 the annual total budget in Scotland was equal to that of one single project in Wales in 1973, the Brenig Valley scheme, and substantially less than the expenditure on the Iron Age site of Gussage All Saints in Dorset in one season.

How could such a situation have been allowed to exist? Was there inertia, apathy, incompetence, or lack of genuine rescue contexts? Or was there a problem at all? Many Scottish archaeologists vigorously denied that there was, and castigated critics from the South for making facile generalisations. Yet, scratching a little deeper the picture changed: stories of missed opportunities abounded from those fundamentally dissatisfied with the existing arrangements, yet often in too junior positions to make their views felt—or too anxious for their own futures to risk such comment in a tightly restricted establishment. There were tales of inertia such as the Kinfauns bridge project, where the contractor's offer to pay the total cost of excavation of a cairn cemetery due for total destruction was ultimately withdrawn after a year's bureaucratic delay. There were the miles of natural gas pipe-trenches in Strathmore that had lain open but unexamined for long periods; and a similar missed opportunity north-east of the Roman fort at Ardoch because it had been decided that 'there was nothing to be found'.

Most serious of all was the failure in Scotland to implement Ancient Monument legislation in the way that had become common elsewhere when archaeological potential within a town centre was logically predicted or actually demonstrated. Such failures there had been in plenty by the end of the 1970s: Elgin, Dumfries, Linlithgow, Dumbarton—and few less explicable than Perth. As one of the country's most important early trading centres with a royal castle and the site of an early parliament house, Perth was a natural candidate for archaeological investigation. Any modern pipe-trench or other disturbance in the plots to the rear of property in the High Street had demonstrated the richness of the organic deposits—indeed, such deposits were observed by the author to a depth of two metres behind 88 High Street in 1972, and from further down the High Street towards the River Tay there had been reports that the mechanical excavation of sewers had shown archaeological deposits reaching a depth of over six metres along the old river frontage. However, the site was not excavated despite a redevelopment that would, under normal circumstances, have been judged a suitable opportunity.

Yet no excavation was conducted at Perth until 1976. It should, however, be pointed out that there was a lack of archaeological personnel at the time, and the limited number was inefficiently deployed. It was symptomatic of such a situation that, on the one hand, the Roman fort at Loudon Hill on the eastern border of Ayrshire could be cited as a classic example of the destruction of a site by quarrying, while, on the other, the excavation in advance of quarrying remained unpublished. Recovery of the near complete plan of the fort by a programme of rescue work over a period of years would have made this site comparable with the fort at Pan Llystyn in Caernarvonshire which had been totally excavated prior to destruction by quarrying in 1965–7.

Until excavations in the 1970s in Glasgow and St Andrews, there had been no urban rescue work in Scottish cities. The rate of urban redevelopment had been as destructive of the pre-Industrial Revolution period as anywhere else in Britain. Prior to 1970–1 virtually no attempt was made by the old Ministry of Public Buildings and Works to watch building sites or recover archaeological material. Indeed in many of the most important burghs, such as Dundee, Stirling and Aberdeen, massive post-War developments had already destroyed a great deal of the archaeological evidence for the history of the towns before the nineteenth century. In the mid-1970s, in addition to major cities such as Glasgow and Edinburgh, many of the smaller burghs, such as Elgin, were threatened by large-scale development schemes.

Against this background the greatest problem was the shortage of archaeologists of sufficient experience, particularly in urban rescue archaeology. Of the eight Scottish universities, one had an archaeologist on its staff who specialised in the post-Roman period. Neither of the two major museums, the National Museum of Antiquities in Edinburgh or the Hunterian Museum in Glasgow, had specialists in this field. In the smaller museums, only Paisley was an exception to this rule. The number of well-established county archaeological societies with a practical programme was small. Probably none had the availability of skilled digging personnel appropriate to maintain rural or urban excavation.

Despite such handicaps, the first urban excavations were conducted in June–July 1969, on the site of Greyfriars in Albion Street, Glasgow, by Eric Talbot of Glasgow University. His programme was designed to test hypotheses about the development of the city centre. Few areas were available for excavation in the medieval core of Glasgow, and particular importance was attached to the Greyfriars site. Documentary evidence had shown that it was the home of the Observant Friars from somewhere between AD 1473 and 1479, until the time of the Reformation. Greyfriars thus offered an opportunity for the recovery of stratified material from a site dated from documentary evidence. Moreover, records from 1820 suggested that the associated cemetery had already been located. The excavations conducted by Talbot suffered from all the assorted problems of urban rescue work, to which was added a new ingredient of Glaswegian gang attack. Nonetheless, the material from the medieval site provided the first occasion in Scotland of medieval finds in an urban context from an archaeological excavation.

More importantly, Talbot laid the foundations for further work in

Glasgow by systematising a plan relating archaeological implications to proposed city-centre developments. Thus, for example, a year later in St Andrews Dr Nicholas Brooks began excavating to the east side of Abbey Street in advance of road-widening. Here, the main structures revealed were a large house of twelfth- to thirteenth-century date, and the sixteenth-century granary of St Leonard's College. Further work in both cities was based on the implication surveys that resulted from these pioneer exploits. As a result of these efforts, in March 1970 the Society of Antiquaries of Scotland, becoming increasingly aware of urban rescue problems, launched a conference on the subject that produced the important publication, *Scotland's Medieval Burghs*, a booklet designed to show planners and archaeologists what was left of medieval archaeology in Scotland's historic towns.

Talbot's pioneer work in Glasgow was conducted in tandem with other excavations. Absence of any finds dated earlier than the sixteenth century on a site in the High Street showed that it was only at that period that the two medieval population nuclei, around the Cathedral and the banks of the Clyde, had coalesced. Elsewhere, at Rotten Row, a medieval trackway was sectioned during extensions to the University of Strathclyde. Talbot was also responsible for the examination of various isolated sites within the Glasgow conurbation. In 1971 he was able to examine, at Pollock in south Glasgow, what was left of the castle—a late medieval tower-house that had already been substantially demolished in 1710. In the same area, the demolition of Castle Milk, built in 1460, provided an opportunity to examine its surviving tower-house.

Further afield, the central core of Dumbarton, which received a charter as early as 1222, claimed attention. Much of the central area of this small medieval town was swept away for a new shopping precinct and a relief road, and excavation of various areas along the High Street next to the River Leven showed that, while the High Street axis was previously the focus of settlement, the existing shape of the town sprang from fifteenth-century expansion into the loop of the river.

Comparable initiatives in Edinburgh were slow in coming. The first rescue excavation in the capital took place in 1973, under the direction of John Schofield, for the Medieval Archaeology Panel of the Cockburn Association. Although the archaeological response was on a scale far from appropriate to the importance of Edinburgh as an archaeological site, it was a first step. Edinburgh is particularly rich in documentary evidence from tax rolls to contemporary etchings, from the late medieval period. Etchings bring out the special nature of the fifteenth-century town running either side of the Royal Mile as it drops from the Castle, past St Giles's Kirk towards the Holyrood area. Five- to seven-storeyed houses fronting the High Street gave direct access to countless 'wynds', or alleys, that led to a series of houses running at right-angles to the main street. At places these houses end abruptly on what is demonstrably the line of the fifteenth-century defensive circuit known as the King's Wall.

Although the 1973 excavations failed to locate the course of the wall with certainty (indeed, sections of it may have been no more than conglomerations of existing property boundaries), the archaeological importance of Edinburgh was shown in other ways. Unique trade contacts with continental sources were revealed: large amounts of Rhineland stoneware were among the discoveries, including one of the largest groups of fifteenth-century types ever excavated in Britain, and Bellarmine jugs from Seigberg and Frechen also figured. This high incidence of foreign material both emphasised the importance of Edinburgh as a medieval commercial centre and constituted a dating agent for local material from other excavations in the city. The importance of the North Sea in forging contact between, rather than dividing, the medieval kingdoms along its shores, has become a major accepted fact of medieval archaeology. Excavations at Bergen, Lund, Ribe, Hamburg, Amsterdam, Antwerp and other continental sites, have shown evidence of trade with Britain during the middle ages. Comparable exploration has been forthcoming on a far smaller scale in Great Britain, least of all in Scotland, where until the 1973 excavations no project had thrown any substantial light on the contribution made by the Scottish kingdom.

Edinburgh, Aberdeen and Dundee are the three principal maritime trading cities of the east coast. At Dundee, as *Scotland's Medieval Burghs* reveals, the old core had, by 1970, already been largely destroyed in archaeological terms by modern redevelopment. Trial excavations within the city in 1973 by Elizabeth Thoms of Dundee Museum confirmed this gloomy conclusion. At Aberdeen, however, the situation was somewhat different. The site was always one of the principal burghs of Scotland, and King David I (1124–53) formally endowed it with the status of a royal borough, although, as at Perth and likewise Montrose, settlement most probably existed on the site long before. Through its trade contacts, both inland and overseas, the town became one of the three wealthiest cities in Scotland in the twelfth century. The actual area of the early burgh was relatively small and dictated by the physical structure of hills clustered close to the mouth of the Dee, which formed the original harbour to south-eastern Scotland.

During the 1970s development accelerated in the city, stimulated by the contemporary oil boom. Until 1973 no archaeological excavations had even taken place within Aberdeen, but in the summer of that year a rescue dig was organised at a site in Broad Street. The project was surprisingly successful in producing large quantities of important material reflecting socio-economic conditions, particularly from the fourteenth century. As at St Andrews, it proved possible to reconstruct some of the plans of the medieval housing, but the justification for the excavation lay, above all, in proving that tangible remains of Aberdeen's archaeological past were accessible when sites were due for redevelopment. The project at Broad Street was the impetus for several others, notably the recovery, in late 1974, of part of a medieval timber-framed quayside at the mouth of the Dee. The remains produced a mass of environmental material which, taken with the surviving pottery, bones and other fragments, served to fill out the picture of everyday life in medieval Aberdeen.

The issues facing the future of urban rescue excavation in Scotland had become clear cut by the end of the 1970s. Knowledge of the origins and growth of medieval towns made enormous progress in southern Britain during that decade, progress that, with certain exceptions such as York, was not reflected north of the Trent. In Scotland in particular, only the first steps were taken along an obviously lengthy path, and many questions remained to be answered. Did the grant of royal status, for example, bring structural changes to a town, or simply represent recognition of earlier development? When were stone walls introduced into the defensive circuits? What was the topography of early Scottish towns—were the tenements and tenement plots comparable with those documentarily attested to in Edinburgh? What part did foreign trade play in the local economy?

If *Scotland's Medieval Burghs* can be said to have erred, it was in the underestimation both of the amount of urban stratified deposits and of their importance in answering such questions. During the early 1970s archaeologists watched the first steps in urban work with growing interest. These confirmed, particularly at Broad Street in Aberdeen, what had long been obvious in, for example, Perth and Edinburgh: that the archaeology of the towns of Scotland could be quite as informative as that elsewhere.

This simple point had a fundamental bearing on contemporary official policies. As long as the Ancient Monuments Acts were not interpreted in Scotland as they were further south, there was the danger that opportunities for major urban rescue work would be missed. During the last decade in England and Wales the demonstration of reasonable probability of surviving archaeological remains in an urban context was taken as the justification for mounting a rescue project. This was not the case in Scotland.

Likewise, the scale of operations in Scotland did not approach that of those further south. One application for urban excavations in the early 1970s requested the paltry sum of £50 from the Scottish Inspectorate! And time and again in Scotland it was argued that the personnel did not exist to cope with excavational problems, and, more obliquely, that the Scottish universities had failed in their duty to produce trained archaeologists. Both arguments were irrelevant. The solution to the problem of staffing on an adequate scale is the introduction of skilled staff from elsewhere, as was, in fact, proved in the Broad Street excavations in Aberdeen.

Urban rescue work with its consequent discoveries among all other archaeological operations, can most effectively fire the public imagination. While it is justifiable that figures such as Ian Crawford should have drawn attention in the 1970s to the amount of coastal erosion in north-east Scotland, or the amount of destruction through afforestation, the prevention of neither of these could lead to the recovery of important information. Only excavation over sufficiently large areas could have produced significant results.

The great drawback to Scottish urban excavation in the 1970s was the scale on which it was conducted. The results of work at Winchester, York or London, which were subsequently taken as commonplace, were only achieved by excavations large in scale and therefore expensive. But since the Scottish Inspectorate was looked to as the major source of funding, there seemed to be a reluctance on the part of the officials concerned to recognise that the predictable recovery of finds in an urban context was a genuine reason for rescue excavation.

Perth was the city where the issues coalesced to provide Scotland with its first major example of an urban rescue excavation, one which far

Fig. 34 The archaeologically destructive effect of coastal erosion, Broch of Gurness, Orkney

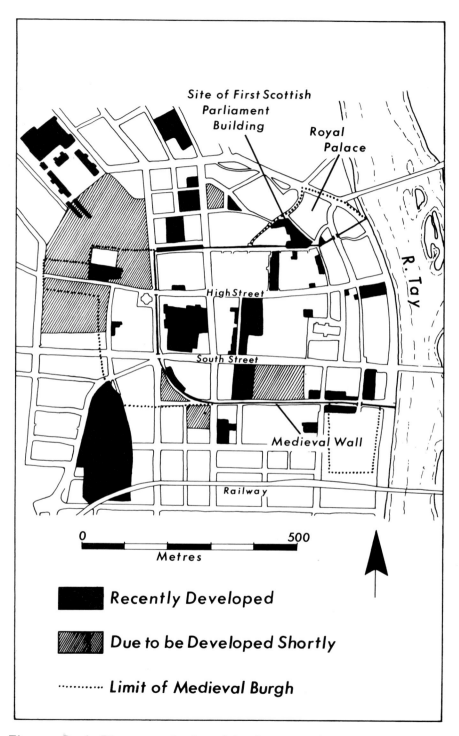

Fig. 35 Perth. Diagrammatic plan of the city centre showing medieval walls

exceeded, both in historical and visual terms, what even its protagonists had envisaged. In retrospect it can be seen that Perth was in fact the Winchester of Scotland—it was a city that had enjoyed a relatively brief period of prosperity at an important time in the development of the Scottish kingdom but which declined in the later Middle Ages. Thus excavation offered an unrivalled opportunity to examine a city of great importance in the eleventh, twelfth and thirteenth centuries.

In the medieval city the settlement was bounded on the east by the River Tay, and the walled quadrangle of the city was divided by two major thoroughfares, South Street and High Street (see Fig. 35). Both these streets are known to have had gates at their west ends by 1180. St John's Kirk, the major church in the area, lay between them to the east, while the royal castle was located beneath the present museum just outside the city walls. It was in this area to the east, close to the Watergate, that the main riverside community flourished: Perth already appeared on the historical scene as a prosperous community early in the twelfth century. It lay at the highest tidal point on the Tay where the river could easily be crossed, and was an important nexus for routes from the Grampians, and from Strathmore running southwards to Fife and the central lowlands.

Most of all, the river gave Perth easy means of communication with the rest of eastern Scotland and, indeed, with the Continent. By the middle of the twelfth century Perth's revenue from ships' customs was more than that of any other Scottish burgh: wine and dyes were imported, and wool and hides were exported. Royal visits furthered the prosperity of the city and of the neighbouring Augustinian monastery at Scone. During the thirteenth century Perth appears to have been the only walled city in Scotland, a reflection of its prosperity and status under royal patronage. Yet the city's prosperity was not prolonged. Perhaps the military campaigns in the area in 1296 and again in 1398 did much to destroy the stability and living standards of the time, and by the late fifteenth century Perth had lost its economic primacy to Edinburgh, Aberdeen and Dundee.

Archaeologically, the attested prosperity and decline of a city at various phases of the medieval period can prove a bonus, since the degree of superimposition and destruction by late medieval and modern buildings is likely to have been limited. At Perth, in the High Street, well away from the river, one redevelopment site in 1975 had shown several metres of well-preserved stratified deposits. These deposits contained much organic material, such as timber and seeds, which does not normally survive in archaeological sites. There had been constant indications from various construction trenches that the surviving stratigraphy actually deepened eastwards towards the river. Indeed, it was suggested that over seven metres of archaeological deposits lay at the end of the High Street, close to the waterfront. Considering the problems that Perth faces from the River Tay and its frequent flooding, it remained for the archaeologists to exploit the rescue situation on a scale sufficient to demonstrate the medieval potential of Perth with such an impact that the message of rescue archaeology would be brought permanently home in Scottish historical centres.

In 1975 excavations began on a test site near St John's Kirk. This limited operation was enough to show the archaeologists concerned, Elizabeth Thoms and Margaret Stewart, that there was great potential. Although the area was limited, so much pottery was recovered that at one stage the normal pottery trays were quite inadequate. Moreover, the organic soils contained a broad range of leather and other preserved items.

With this evidence, large-scale excavation began in December 1975 under the direction of Nicholas Bogden, Director of the Perth Archaeological Unit. The first part of the programme was the recovery of the wall and ditch of medieval Perth which had probably been slighted in 1312 when Robert the Bruce recaptured the town from the English. This major discovery fuelled the case for examining much more of the adjacent area in the High Street, where documentary evidence suggested the old 'parliament house', believed to have been totally destroyed in 1816, had stood. The team rapidly came across the remains of the building. It proved to be a late sixteenth-century town house that had served both as a temporary meeting place for a Scottish parliament (probably in 1606) and for a number of other secular and religious uses. The stratigraphic position of the house was perhaps its most important feature. It had sealed very substantial archaeological deposits beneath its cellars, primarily consisting of exceptionally well-preserved wattle-and-daub buildings of the thirteenth century, separated by paths and middens. Up until the discovery of these birchwood wattle structures practically nothing had been known of Scottish vernacular architecture before the fifteenth century.

The remarkable preservation of objects and environmental evidence in the soil placed the newly recovered material in a special category in Scottish archaeology. The finds included wooden bowls, and their existence explained some of the gaps in the kinds of local and imported pottery discovered. The well-preserved ironwork included a full range of medieval spears, arrowheads and even a battle-axe. The excavations also yielded over one hundred samples of thirteenth- and fourteenth-century textiles, amongst which two exceptional pieces of lace in particular, dating from about 1300, indicated the relative prosperity of the burgh at that time. And quantities of shoes confirmed the previously-known fact that this quarter along the High Street was particularly associated with skinners and leather-workers.

Fig. 36 Perth. An aerial view of the River Tay with the High Street running down to the river

Fig. 37 A fragment of lace from *c*.1300 discovered near the 'parliament house', Perth 1976

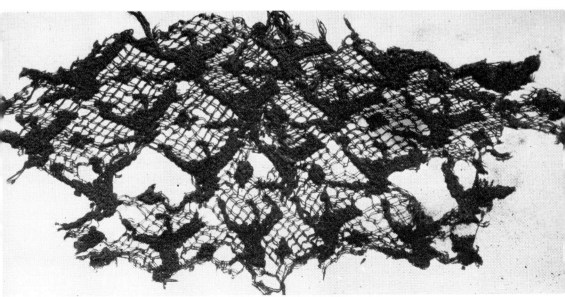

While full publication of the Perth excavations is still awaited, the richness of these finds revolutionised public expectations of what could be achieved by urban rescue archaeology in Scotland's historic cities, and at about the same time there were other developments that rapidly led to progress on the Scottish archaeological scene. The Royal Commission for Ancient and Historic Monuments received an increase in staff to cover additional work in advance of afforestation throughout Great Britain, and the effectiveness of the Scottish Inspectorate was greatly increased since officials were given specific problems, such as historic cities, coastal erosion, pipelines and afforestation, to tackle. By 1977 the need for a mobile excavation team was recognised by the creation of a Central Excavation Unit for Scotland, housed at Falkirk and deployed to the more important rescue projects, such as Huntingtower and various pipe-line and road construction projects.

These developments had effect: the following years saw excavations at Dunfermline, Falkirk, Dunbar and Perth again. But while the funding of Scottish archaeology had improved considerably by the end of the decade, it was still in receipt of only six or seven per cent of the total rescue archaeology grant available for the United Kingdom. For the period 1977–8 a single unit in one English centre received £110,000, while the total for the whole of Scotland was only £142,000. If based on the normal criteria for the distribution of government funds, this figure would have been (since Scotland comprises over one third of Britain's area) substantially over one quarter of a million pounds.

In Scotland, North Sea Oil and related developments brought in their train the construction of pipelines, industrial sites and housing estates. These developments, in one way or another, affected parts of the archaeology of the Scottish seaboard, which, moreover, has always been particularly susceptible to erosion of its coastal sites such as Buckhoy in the north. The need in Scotland was, therefore, for the continuing improvement of archaeological facilities, and most notably for permanent archaeological posts. However, by the end of the 1970s there had been little change in the number of posts available, and those in the Central Excavation Unit were even cut. Unlike England and Wales, where practically every county has one or more archaeologists on its staff, only two local authority archaeologists work in Scotland, one in Tayside and one in Grampian. This has meant greater strain on the central authorities, but the Scottish Inspectorate have responded mainly by creating several temporary posts to tackle problems of pipelines or afforestation. More permanent posts mean more money, and that, unfortunately, has not been forthcoming in Scotland.

9
London and York

London

> Finally we may refer to the lament, explicit and implicit in the volume, that the destruction of Roman remains in London by deep excavation for modern building is proceeding faster than the building up of construction record by exact observation. We can never know all we wish to know of Roman London, but much, essential to our understanding of its history, is daily being destroyed. If funds were available it would be possible to maintain a close watch on deep excavations; the stratification of the Roman city thus exposed could be fully recorded, and the objects scattered through the Roman levels preserved. Work on these lines is being done today, but under great and increased difficulty. The merchants of so wealthy a city could well spare an annual sum sufficient to secure the preservation of the relics of its early history as from time to time they are exhumed.
>
> Sir Cyril Fox, *Antiquity* III, 10 (1929, p. 242).

These words have a surprisingly modern ring to them although they were written as long ago as 1928. They had, at that time, little effect on the work of recording the archaeological remains of London's past. Before 1946 any archaeological work in the City of London was normally limited solely to observation, or what archaeologists called 'watching briefs', of the construction of deep cellars and other such structural work. This had major successes: much of the line of the city wall and substantial fragments of the Roman basilica were located in this way. Although considerable archaeological evidence was found in this way, there was no disguising the way in which the sheer predominance of *Roman* remains had led to an imbalance in the archaeological knowledge of London's past. Apart from a record of the walls of Leadenhall, for instance, observed as long ago as 1881, information about the early and later medieval city, its walls and churches, remained at a relatively minor level.

Bombing in 1940–1 caused great damage in the City of London, and after the War, the archaeological potential of the damage was noted. In 1946 the Roman and Medieval London Excavation Council was established with Professor W. F. Grimes as its Director of Excavations. Their most famous discoveries were from the Roman period. The excavators uncovered an early second-century fort, the ramparts of which pre-dated the city wall but were later partly incorporated in it, giving the circuit its curious appearance in the north-western sector. In 1954 the Walbrook Mithraeum with its marble sculptures and other art treasures was unearthed. The discovery aroused unprecedented interest in the remains of London's past. Unfortunately, however, it also marked a turn for the worse in the relationship between archaeologists and developers—the latter ultimately paid for the delay imposed by public interest in the outstanding nature of the archaeological discoveries. Professor Grimes's major achievements in the medieval period were the archaeological investigation of St Bride's church, and the re-dating of the hollow bastions on the city wall from the Roman period to the thirteenth century.

The boom in bomb-site excavation ended in 1962 with the winding up of the Roman and Medieval London Excavation Council. It had achieved some remarkable discoveries but it is perhaps best judged in a modern context by the fact that, in the 18 years of its existence, it had raised a mere £46,000. The scale of its financial support had therefore been wholly inappropriate to the archaeological problems posed by the City of London, and the point was underlined by the total subvention of a paltry £850 for Professor Grimes's publication, *Excavations in Roman and Medieval London* (1968). By present-day standards these post-war excavations were conducted on shoe-string budgets, and were made possible only by the availability of volunteers and the sufferance of the developers.

In the 1960s the Guildhall Museum, which was responsible for archaeology in the City of London prior to the creation of the Museum of London, continued its watching briefs on building sites. One of these, in combination with limited excavation, led to the discovery of what is claimed to be the Governor's residence on the eastern side of Cannon Street station, and of a Flavian bath suite in Upper Thames Street. By this time the City was entering a phase of massive redevelopment in areas largely unaffected by war damage, but in the early 1970s the Guildhall Museum still had but a single field officer to cope with the situation. In view of the legal hiatus whereby a developer could prevent prior archaeological investigation, excavation was possible only on sites where the City of London Corporation itself acted as developer. This was the case in Billingsgate where a late Roman house and Dark Age material were recovered. Nevertheless, in 1965, under conditions of great difficulty, Brian Philp, who organised a group of volunteer diggers from Kent, was also able to gain access to a private development east of Gracechurch Street and there uncovered part of the forum and its Flavian predecessor.

These rare discoveries, where access had combined with the existence of significant stratified deposits, had, by 1970, served to suggest the importance of what little might remain. But by then half the forum area and half the site of the Leadenhall residence had already been archaeologically destroyed. The amphitheatre and theatre, and likewise the imperial temple that London must have contained, have never been located. Even the Roman town plan is less understood than that of any other major town in Roman Britain. Yet public interest has automatically centred on our knowledge of the city in the Roman period because the depth and massive structure of many Roman remains renders them more easily recognisable. The resulting focus on the Roman period meant that, while it has been possible to show the development of the Roman city at various stages between the first and fourth centuries, no such confidence was, until very recently, extended to the demonstration of the development sequence within any other major historical phase. In academic terms the problem centres on the way in which the late Roman town-plan evolved into that of the Middle Ages.

Anglo-Saxon London was uncharted, partly because it has aroused only academic interest, and partly because it was largely timber-built. Yet, just as Tacitus, the Roman historian, described London as 'crowded with traders', and 'a great centre of commerce', so the British historian Bede referred to it as the 'mart of many nations resorting to it by land and sea'. Thus the riverside port and its industries played a key role in the city's development, from its early days, but it is not known if the river frontage was defended at the time of the Viking raids. The strata that can answer questions like this do not always survive. Not only have eighteenth- and nineteenth-century cellars often carried them away, but, in terms of archaeological stratigraphy, each age has helped destroy traces of its immediate predecessor. The pits and wells of medieval London have destroyed much pre-Conquest stratigraphy. Likewise, post-medieval reconstruction has removed so much evidence of everyday buildings in medieval London that there is little hope of identifying an ordinary medieval timber-framed house. Only the churches and certain other sites such as palaces, survive.

Destruction has been rampant. London has been occupied since at least AD 43, yet the physical remains of its first 1300 years is both limited and dwindling. In the present City of London, an area slightly larger than the Roman walled area, incorporating many of the extra-mural cemeteries, one quarter has already been archaeologically destroyed by, for instance, the building of basements and railways. Shallower basements and foundations have damaged a further 58 per cent, at least to the upper Roman levels. This leaves 118 acres theoretically lying available for potential archaeology within the City. But theoretical and practical availability for excavation are different. The pace of redevelopment has been such that 435 acres within the City were redeveloped in three decades following the War. At this speed a mere

Fig. 38 Visscher's view of the London waterfront (1616)

two decades would be required to redevelop the remaining available land. Out of the total area of 667 acres, public buildings, churches and other monuments account for 20, and any future archaeological information would have to derive from the 22 remaining acres of open space.

By the 1970s it was clear to the archaeological world that the situation could not continue as it was. In the City of London one field officer was having to cope with a situation for which a growing rescue archaeological unit was still inadequate in 1974, as well as Southwark where another unit now exists. With the arrival of Max Hebditch as Curator of the Guildhall Museum in 1972 there was the opportunity for change. That change was due in many respects to the Baynard's Castle affair, where severe public criticism had emphasised the inadequate archaeological facilities within the City. Documentary evidence has amply shown that east of Blackfriars Bridge and the Mermaid Theatre must have lain the site of Baynard's Castle, the Norman fortress guarding the upper end of the port of London, and containing its own docks and quays. Yet the ground lay derelict for two years before contract work actually began in 1972. The howls of public protest when the anticipated remains appeared precipitated a confrontation between developer and archaeologist, and one that could, and should, have been avoided by adequate forward planning on both sides. Though some important material was recovered from the piecemeal excavation that ensued, and the evidence of trade connections from the infilled dock was important, this did not wholly compensate for the inadequate excavation of the structure itself amidst the reconstruction work. From the

FLUVIUS

South Warke

time of this salvage work on the Baynard's Castle site, it was clear that archaeological organisation had to be strengthened.

The subsequent changes were the direct result of two-pronged pressure, from the Guildhall Museum itself and from Rescue. Although the two parties never quite spoke in unison concerning the scale of objective, they offered a classic demonstration of the value of two pressure groups operating simultaneously, one from within, the other from without. At the time the City of London authorities gave a mere £4,000–£5,000 for rescue archaeology in the whole of the City area. The authorities did not relish the public comments by Rescue on the inadequacy of the arrangements (the Lord Mayor of the time threatened legal action), and they were also faced with equivalent criticism from Museum officials. The key to the Rescue campaign lay in the 1973 publication of *The Future of London's Past* that set an entirely new standard for archaeological implications reports on this scale. The authors concluded that there existed only 15–20 years of archaeological work left within the City.

These words were in effect no stronger than those of the Guildhall Museum's own publication, addressed largely to developers and to the City authorities. In the latter Max Hebditch stated bluntly that . . .

> the rebuilding of those areas of the city that were unaffected by war damage provides an opportunity to solve by archaeological means many of the outstanding problems connected with the early history of the city . . . If this opportunity is not grasped now it will be lost forever . . . In the absence of antiquities legislation comparable to many other countries, success in seizing this opportunity depends upon the co-operation of developers, archaeologists and planners.

The implication of both reports was that archaeology conducted to modern professional standards costs money, and that, in the context of a city centre, it may cost developers both time and money. The strength of the reports lay in the fact that one was backed up with a formidable body of meticulous documentation and scholarship, and the other was written by an insider. The overlay maps of *The Future of London's Past* allowed anybody, developer or otherwise, to discover easily and quickly what any building programme would mean in archaeological terms. Small wonder that sales were brisk in the property world. *The Future of London's Past* went on to suggest that a permanent staff of 74 was needed to conduct excavations and carry out research and publication at a cost of £185,000 per annum. These figures were criticised as being too high—and certainly must have shocked those who believed that the figure of about £4,000 a year contributed by the City of London was adequate—but the requirements were based on the pace of development and the proven costs of running a research unit at Winchester. Furthermore, the case was admitted in effect by a member of the Guildhall staff, quoted in *Guildhall*, the Corporation of London newspaper, November 1973, when he commented that if they were permitted to excavate all the sites that merited it, they could need £100,000 per annum to keep up with the one per cent ($6\frac{3}{4}$ acres) of the heart of London being reconstructed annually.

Progress was forthcoming, however, if not on the scale urged by Rescue. Late in 1973 the City of London Corporation had appointed Brian Hobley to the post of Chief Urban Archaeologist in control of a permanent archaeological research party. Essentially his job was to direct a number of individual archaeological teams dealing with specific sites and their publication. One, for instance, worked on the results of the Baynard's Castle operation, another excavated the Custom House and Wool Quay, while a third later excavated around St Paul's. By the end of 1973 the overall budget had increased tenfold to £40,000, of which the City of London was contributing more than half.

Armed with the evidence from *The Future of London's Past* for the depth of archaeological deposits, rapid progress was subsequently made. Archaeological deposits of great depth lie along the old course of the Walbrook, because, over the centuries, the river bed silted up and the land above levelled. If basements have not destroyed it, the evidence is also deep on the City's two hills, Cornhill and Ludgate. The prime area for deposits, however, lies along the waterfront where there has been relatively little development this century and where the river frontage has moved out since the Roman period, thus encapsulating a mass of earlier river frontage and relics of trade and everyday life preserved in deep organic deposits. In the area of the waterfront along Upper Thames Street, for instance, as in comparable areas of York, the waterlogged ground has preserved timber and other organic material which would long since have decayed in another environment.

Brian Hobley's team achieved notable results in a number of excavations along the river frontage. At the New Fresh Wharf fragments of a timber-built boat from the twelfth century or earlier were uncovered. The boat lay next to the remains of successive medieval and Roman waterfronts, and pottery from the overlying deposits that sealed the boat in position indicated that it could not be later than twelfth-century in date, and may perhaps have belonged to the period preceding the Norman Conquest. The boat consisted of a series of pine planks whose overlaps were held by wooden pegs made watertight by moss. No other example of similar construction is known from anywhere in north-western Europe. The intricate and meticulous process of raising the fragments of timber was completed in 1975, and each section was carefully cleaned and drawn in the Guildhall Museum.

The boat itself proved not to be the only feature of interest. The area of Roman waterfront examined is the most substantial yet uncovered in London. Its proximity to the site of London Bridge (finally located early in 1982) would have made it a highly developed part of the first Roman fort. The quantity of Samian pottery imported in the first and second centuries AD demonstrates the sophistication of its trade. The date of the

Fig. 39 Trig Lane, London. The timberwork of the medieval quay has been preserved by its waterlogged condition

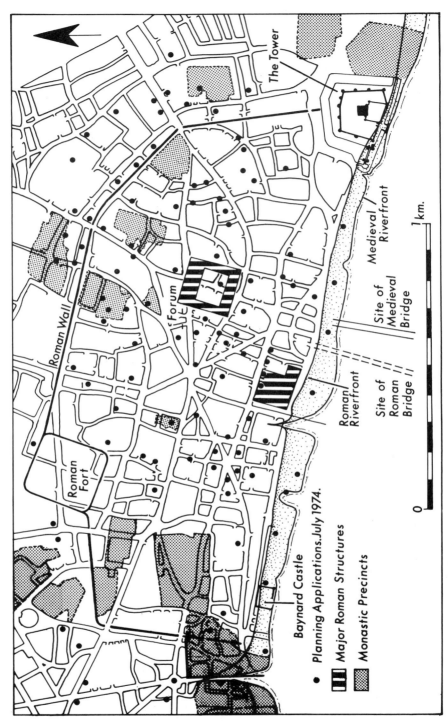

Fig. 40 The City of London. Diagrammatic plan showing major Roman structures and monastic precincts. The dots indicate redevelopment projects under consideration in the mid-1970s

128

waterfront's construction lies in the second half of the second century and the form is that of a timber box-frame—large squared oak piles driven into the ground and jointed at right angles with tiers of beams, cross-tied at the front. In comparison the early medieval waterfront was less substantial: a revetment of timber and rubble rested on a foundation or matting of small branches embedded in a clay spread. The latter sealed the top of the protruding Roman timber structures that had still survived. The purpose of the matting must have been to act as an area onto which boats might be hauled at low tide. Such results showed the value of excavation where stratigraphic deposits survive in London. The only sites comparable with New Fresh Wharf are those at Xanten in Germany, and the Custom House site in the City that Brian Hobley's team investigated. At the latter, another fine second-century Roman wharf was uncovered, again sealed by similar remains from the medieval period.

The question of whether there existed a formal riverside defence, as opposed to wharfage, in the Roman period was finally settled in 1975 when 130 metres of wall were uncovered beside the Mermaid Theatre. The wall proved not to be contemporary with the third-century land-walls but dated instead to the late fourth century, when the Roman general Stilicho attempted to stiffen the defences of a disintegrating Roman province. The wall had been hurriedly assembled by re-using the stones of earlier structures. One group of re-used stones belonged to

Fig. 41 A Roman mosaic floor being cleaned and prepared for lifting and eventual display at the Museum of London

a monumental screen depicting pagan deities. Another group derived from a single portalled monumental archway approximately eight metres long by six metres high, and provided the rare opportunity of reconstructing a complete example of Roman monumental building in Britain.

After 1975 the focus of excavation shifted away from the Roman and medieval waterfront and the range of discovery broadened: a late Roman inhumation cemetery at St Bartholomew's, Saxon *grubenhausen* (sunken-floor dwellings) at five other sites, and larger late Saxon structures at the GPO site near St Paul's. After the Norman period it is not uncommon for documentary evidence to be available for the archaeologist and thus Brian Hobley's team were able to refine their objectives considerably when considering this period up until the Great Fire of 1666, which left a well-defined burnt layer on many sites. Information about ordinary dwellings and tenements was sorely lacking until recently when it begun to emerge from behind the medieval waterfront. From the other end of the social scale, much was ultimately recovered, not from the destroyed interior of Baynard's Castle, but from the nearby dock where the royal tailors threw unwanted fragments of cloth. And in 1978–9 the south-western corner of Henry VIII's Bridewell Palace was uncovered, with the massive foundations to counteract the unstable subsoil beside the neighbouring River Fleet.

Large scale excavation is continuing in the City and so there is hope for the future of archaeology in London. Since 1974 it can be claimed that no site of known archaeological importance has failed to be examined before redevelopment. At the same time under the present system there is no doubt that archaeology remains a waif. Where excavation is necessary the deployment of a professionally directed team using all modern techniques to excavate the largest areas possible is required. Such a team requires the support of specialists, including, particularly on the waterfront sites, workers in other disciplines such as zoologists and botanists to reconstruct the past environment. Above all, excavation needs time and the legal teeth to secure access as a matter of course. Figure 40 shows planning applications formally made in a typical year in the mid-1970s. The sheer size of some of these developments (although several have been delayed) comes as a shock within an area already so highly redeveloped. Yet in general terms the more extensive an area examined the greater the value of the archaeological in-formation recovered. And as this book has emphasised, modern building methods inevitably destroy the bulk of archaeological deposits to a depth of six metres or so within the area of the City of London.

For the best part of two decades following the discovery of the Mithras temple in 1954, developers of any project of this scale regularly

Fig. 42 Excavation at the GPO site near St Paul's London

spent a larger sum of money on subsoil survey than that required for the total excavation of the area by archaeological means. The forced delay between demolition and reconstruction inevitably cost developers money in time. Because of the premium on space, and the cost of land itself, London has always been the test case for the development of any archaeological legislation. In 1972 the Secretary of State for the Environment suggested that legislation be brought forward to ensure that time for excavation would be provided prior to redevelopment. Such an Act finally materialised in 1979, but implementation in London is yet to be seen.

York

In London considerations of building conservation play practically no part in the questions underlying rescue archaeology. There are other historic centres where conservation of above ground buildings plays a vital part in the shaping of overall redevelopment policy. Perhaps this is truer of no place more than of the city of York. The background to such a situation was Lord Esher's report *York, a Study in Conservation* (HMSO, 1968). The Esher report advocated an attempt to preserve the worthwhile within the walled perimeter of York, and to create alongside this, dwelling areas that would transform the derelict centre into a pleasant urban environment. Fundamental to the plan was the assumption that all but indigenous traffic would be excluded from the city nucleus, and the outer ring road scheme was a practical result.

While the Esher report was certainly to be welcomed on many grounds, it created a radically new problematic situation for archaeology in York. The agreed line of a proposed *inner* ring road was to cut across no less than six Romano-British cemetery areas, two Roman suburbs, areas of Anglo-Saxon or Viking occupation, three large medieval suburbs, and the documented locations of one priory, several churches, hospitals and almshouses. The proposal was ultimately abandoned, although it may well be revived in a future period of economic growth.

At the same time, crucial to the Esher plan was the area known as the Aldwark on the eastern side of the medieval city perimeter. Even relatively shallow foundations there are likely to encounter archaeological remains, both of an industrial area beyond the limits of the Roman legionary fortress proper, and of documented structures from the Anglo-Saxon or Viking phase. While the development of the Aldwark provided a large area of demonstrable archaeological potential, within the city centre big development projects have been in hand on a number of important sites.

From AD 71 York was the base of the Ninth Legion and retained its major role as a military, administrative and communications centre at

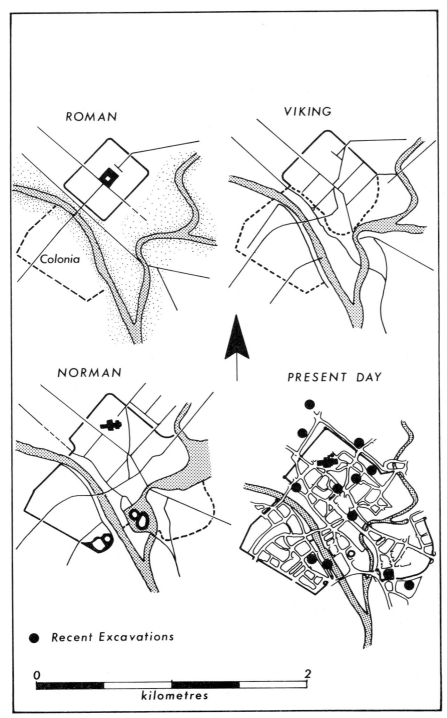

ROMAN

VIKING

Colonia

NORMAN

PRESENT DAY

● Recent Excavations

0   2
kilometres

Fig. 43   York. Diagrammatic plan showing the development of the site in the
Roman, Viking, Norman and present-day periods

various times since, while adding that of a major ecclesiastical centre from the earliest days of Christianity in England. The Roman period in its military phase is represented by the survival of the north-eastern, north-western and south-western walls of the legionary fortress as incorporated in the later city circuit. In the early third century York's importance was on a grander scale when from AD 208–211 Septimius Severus used it as his base for the campaigns against the Caledonian tribes. York served as the capital of the Roman Empire until Severus died there in February 211, and military sources imply the existence of an imperial residence used for administration. Nothing is known of these arrangements in archaeological terms; relatively little of the internal layout of a legionary fortress has been located and such outstanding features as the amphitheatre are still undiscovered.

As part of the general refurbishing of the North a century later, Constantius Chlorus rebuilt the famous riverside defences with their multangular towers when he too resided in York as junior Emperor. Organised Roman military control had ended around the close of the fourth century and clearly some of the old fortress buildings remained standing and in use, whatever their new role.

By the middle Saxon period historical references make it clear that York was already an important ecclesiastical seat and an entrepôt that, as a result of the navigable River Ouse, boasted connections with many Continental ports. From AD 866, when York was occupied by the Vikings, and from AD 919–954 when it flourished as the capital of a Viking kingdom, the picture has become somewhat clearer. The key role of York continued as the site of William I's first castle in the North. Ultimately two castles were required to secure the Norman stronghold and, whatever form the shadowy 'harrowing' of the North may have taken, York assumed the place of England's second city.

This is the context within which the rescue archaeology of York had to be considered. Excavation had been regularly conducted in York for several decades. It is true to say, however, that the bulk of that work centred on the defences, and particularly on the interpretation of the Roman phases. Then, during the stabilisation of the foundations of the Minster, a marvellous technical feat of excavation was conducted by Dr Hope Taylor, Herman Ramm and Derek Philips, which revealed the plans of two successive Norman minsters. The first was erected by Archbishop Thomas of Bayeux (1070–1100), and was succeeded a century later by the second, an even larger building erected by Archbishop Roger of Pont L'Évêque (1154–81). This major archaeological breakthrough served to highlight the relative ignorance of Norman building of a domestic character within the town proper. Despite occasional hints in literary sources, developments immediately subsequent to Roman control have been understood from the results of archaeology alone. With the existence of greater documenatry evidence from the twelfth century onwards there is room for inter-related work between archaeologists and architectural historians to establish the detailed topography and the property boundaries within the late medieval period—problems that subsequent excavations began to tackle.

The Minster excavation was, however, a highly specialised operation, specifically limited to a chosen area. What lent new impetus to rescue work within York was the Esher Report, and, in response, 1972 saw the formation of the York Archaeological Trust for excavation and research, financed by a grant from the Department of the Environment, with other grants from the City of York and the County. The Trust's first Director, Peter Addyman, moved from a lectureship at Southampton University to take up the post. Addyman was born in York and his personal involvement lent edge to the challenge. Yet he took a very considerable professional gamble: in its first year the excavational programme nearly collapsed through a cutback in funding by the Department of the Environment.

Addyman's policy of establishing close relations with the city planning department and construction agents resulted in long advance warning of redevelopment programmes, but nonetheless a major problem stemmed from the sheer bulk and nature of the archaeological deposits that he was rapidly uncovering. One of Addyman's most notable archaeological achievements, based on working large-scale areas, was the identification and excavation of archaeological deposits belonging to the Viking period and preserved to a remarkable degree. Above all he encountered organic deposits on such a scale within York as to demand radically improved processing facilities, so that an environmental laboratory was subsequently established at the nearby University. And had work begun on the projected inner ring road it would have demanded the establishment of a specialist staff to cope with the thousands of graves that would have been encountered, offering a unique record of the trends in national physique and disease from the Roman period onwards.

Archaeological discoveries in York following the foundation of the Trust provided a wide variety of information. In 1974–5, for example, the excavation of the famous south-western defences with their multangular towers prior to the development of a new site in the Forum Bar (in which the foundations of a tower are now preserved), showed that the existing roadway of the legionary fortress had continued in use into the fifth century. But the shortcomings of the framework within which rescue archaeology was conducted had been demonstrated by work elsewhere within the fortress area in 1972–3. The Shepherd Development Company Ltd had allowed examination beneath their development site

Fig. 44 A major Roman sewer discovered during redevelopment, York

of the Talbot Hotel, and, as a result, Roman buildings still standing up to three metres high were identified. However, the Equitable Assets Company Ltd had refused access prior to their reconstruction project when they located the remains of a major Roman sewer system in the northern part of the fortress that necessitated the redesigning of the modern building's proposed foundations. Peter Addyman received an anonymous tip-off about the sewer's existence and a brief period of access was negotiated allowing him and Derek Phillips of the York Minster Excavation Committee two weeks to examine the area. Their work on the surviving Roman buildings demonstrated that a substantial bath-house had been located, and one whose shell had remained in use until the medieval period.

In a city as historically rich as York, there is the additional archaeological factor of a rising water table that has preserved an accumulation of two thousand years of debris in what is, by archaeological standards, near-perfect conditions. York's archaeological unit has proved one of the few such units with the resources, manpower, and scientific skills to attempt tackling the problem. The city can claim to have been the first urban area in Britain which offered a number of integrated scientific analyses to help construct a socio-economic picture from archaeological excavation on a scale that is without parallel in this country. Since 1975 there has been, for instance, excavation not only of the Roman sewer system, but also of a Viking leather workshop, as well as in a church and graveyard at St Helens on the walls abandoned by the sixteenth century.

The importance of the work on the Roman sewer at York was that, in the first place, sufficient lengths were uncovered to identify part of the associated Roman street grid and the position of a major Roman bath-building; and, in the second, analyses of the sludge from the sewer indentified two principal types of beetle, the grain beetle and golden spider beetle (which was erroneously thought to have reached this country from Southern Russia only in the last century), the presence of which shows that a granary had been in close proximity. From such minutiae conclusions were drawn. Moreover, from the absence of normal outdoor faunal remains, entomologists concluded that the water system had been derived from a sealed flow. Further analysis suggested that its source lay in oak woodland on magnesium limestone. The varieties of ant also located in the sludge showed that the temperature of the sewer had been in the region of 70° Fahrenheit, a heat created by the effluent from the nearby legionary baths. Such is the interpretive and prognostic value of environmental archaeology today.

In its present state, archaeology has always been likely to make the greatest contribution in the post-Roman period. The excavation in 1975–6 on the site of a new basement for Lloyds Bank uncovered deposits from the tenth-century tannery. The great depth of the stratified deposits revealed much. The tanners and leather-workers had lived in wattle-and-daub structures riddled with woodworm and death-watch beetle. From the deposits it was evident that the workers had transported the skins inside the shop to strip off fat and hair so that these had ended up in liberal quantities all over the rising floor levels. Fat from the skins had fed a large quantity of maggots in one corner of the room. Such discoveries are made by a process known as wet sieving, and involving flotation with a paraffin/water solution. It enabled archaeologists to show that an elderberry extract had been used to help in the curing of the skins. Also found were the remains of a wooden stretching-frame on which the leather had been treated with woodash prior to stretching, and traces of heather that had probably been used to dye the finished product. On examination under an electron microscope it was seen that the type of wool used derived from flocks similar to the modern merino sheep and therefore imported. Even the whetstones were imports from Scandinavia.

The excavation of cemeteries presented Peter Addyman with a first-class opportunity to examine the earlier population of the city and above all that population's diseases and mortality rate. If pursued on a sufficient scale, such excavation can lead to a demographic history of an urban centre. Addyman was forced to choose from among a bewildering number in York that were destined for destruction. Minute examination, measurement, and collation of bone material have made it possible to compare the human remains and the skeleton information from the presumably more affluent persons buried in the Minster cemetery with, for example, that of the rural population from the nearby deserted medieval village of Wharram Percy. Work in 1967 revealed that the bodies buried within the church tended to be larger and healthier because they belonged to people with sufficient wealth to avoid rickets and general malnutrition. Indeed, a common feature of the tibia that have been found in graves outside the churches is 'Harris' Lines'. Revealed by X-rays of the bone structure, these defects are particularly associated with arrested growth resulting from starvation and hardship.

In the late seventies the Archaeological Trust devoted most of its attention to Coppergate, a trading quarter in the Viking city. The Lloyds Bank excavation had made it clear that York—or Jórvik to give it its Viking name—could produce results of the greatest archaeological and historical importance. Jórvik was, after all, the principal Scandinavian *entrepôt* in Britain. Accordingly, when long-term re-development was planned for the site at the confluence of the Ouse and the Fosse, known as Coppergate, in the heart of medieval York, large-scale excavations were begun and had spectacular results. The archaeol-

Fig. 45 The Coppergate site, York

ogists could guess that the occupation deposits along the 'Street of the Wood-Turners' would reach a depth of 10 metres, and that much of those lower deposits might be waterlogged. So, at a cost of £76,000, and much of it derived from a Scandinavian bank loan (reflecting the interest from abroad in Jórvik), steel shoring was rammed around the edge of the site to make deep excavation possible in the waterlogged conditions—and to protect the adjoining buildings from collapse!

After months of work on the later Viking levels, Richard Hall, the excavation director, found his hopes exceeded by the discovery, in 1979, of three timber-built Viking workshops lying perpendicular to the street front. They were the first such Viking structures to be found in Britain, and the metres of accumulated debris had preserved them in a remarkable state with their collapsed gables and standing solid oak walls. The constructional details were minutely preserved. The massive timber planking had been set on sills and pinned horizontally on massive oak uprights. Two silver coins showing Ethelred the Unready, found in the timber floor, dated the structures to the later tenth century, some time after AD 954 when the last Scandinavian King of Jórvik, Erik Blood-Axe, was expelled and the city passed to the English Crown. A die for an Anglo-Saxon penny was found in one of the buildings, revealing the handiwork of the *frothric*—the moneyer whose name was spelt out in a mirror image on a lead strip that served as a moneyer's trial punch. The other name to appear on this die was that of 'Eadwig Rex'—King Eadwig who held the English throne from AD 955 to 959, immediately after the expulsion of Erik Blood-Axe. Such finds fused the gap between archaeology and history, while the thousands of other objects recovered from Coppergate, ranging from wood chippings to saddle-bows, from jet pendants to carved grave-slabs, revolutionised archaeological knowledge of contemporary trade between Britain and the Continent.

Even in its early stages the excavation of Coppergate more than doubled the number of known Viking objects in the whole of Britain, and when fully published its place will be secure in the history of the achievements of British archaeology. It confirmed the importance of rescue archaeology in York, and alone justified the continuing process of establishing archaeological units in Britain's major historical cities. By 1980 the York Archaeological Trust had a budget in excess of £100,000 per year. The city's stratified deposits made it essential to co-ordinate a technical team capable of integrating simultaneously scientific examination with archaeology. The archaeologists, inevitably inexpert in specialised fields, are served by an on-the-spot scientific presence which identifies the significance of the deposits with which they are dealing, and which they might otherwise overlook. The importance of the introduction of this scheme in York is not that new techniques were being used, but that methods and techniques established for several years were at last being applied to the excavation process in an integrated fashion. The establishment of the environmental laboratory and co-operation with Bradford University provides some of the essential back-up through the application of advanced techniques with equipment beyond the purse of archaeology under normal circumstances.

In this respect, by the end of the 1970s York was perhaps approaching closer to a state of 'total archaeology' than any other site in the country, partly as a result of the drive and personality of those involved and also of the guaranteed presence of stratified deposits in most of the walled

Fig. 46 Emphasis on catching public attention and support at Coppergate, York

area and much of its adjuncts. In moments of despair Peter Addyman could ask what to do when faced with at least 90 acres of archaeological deposits reaching a depth of 10 metres at many points. But more money is always necessary: by the time of its later seasons, the excavation of Coppergate was partly starved of funds and had to be supported to a considerable extent by donations from the public who thronged to visit the site, and from Scandinavian sources that saw the overall importance of the work at Jórvik. Yet by 1980–1 when the penultimate season of excavation was planned at Coppergate, for many reasons it was possible to say that rescue archaeology in Britain was already in relative decline.

10
The Age of Reason?

Since 1969 British archaeology has undergone one of its most rapid periods of change and expansion. Perhaps it was only by the late 1970s when the pace of change slackened that one could begin to see the outline of the new shape that had evolved. The realisation of the 1970s that redevelopment of whatever kind offered archaeologists an opportunity to extract information on an unprecedented scale had, undoubtedly, a major impact. That impact is now more fully appreciated than ever before, and the concept of rescue archaeology has become publicly accepted.

Yet this public advance was not accompanied by a rationalisation of policies and organisations. Confusion was manifest in contrary developments: while many saw the need for radical change, what was sometimes termed 'amateur backlash' blocked attempts in 1975 to form some kind of professional body to guarantee standards of competence among practising archaeologists. The very term 'archaeologists' has been used with such wide connotations that it has even been applied at times to treasure hunters with their metal detectors, the very antithesis of professional archaeology. Yet archaeologists have in part only themselves to blame for lack of accredited standing since they have failed to establish a professional institute. For this reason, significantly, the widely distributed body of American archaeologists still lack creditable corporate entity.

The promise of major change could only centre on the Inspectorate for Ancient Monuments and other official agencies, such as the Royal Commission, harmonising policy between national and local government interests. Above all, legislative change could only be forthcoming from a Department of Environment initiative. The Ancient Monuments Act 1939, the Treasure Trove Law, and the Town and Country Planning Acts all needed revision. Draft versions of a bill to secure adequate provision for urban excavation had been in circulation for years without any sign of the parliamentary time that it deserved.

With committees proliferating and central government policy (particularly in relation to local authority funding) shifting, one might have been forgiven for believing that British archaeology in the 1970s had

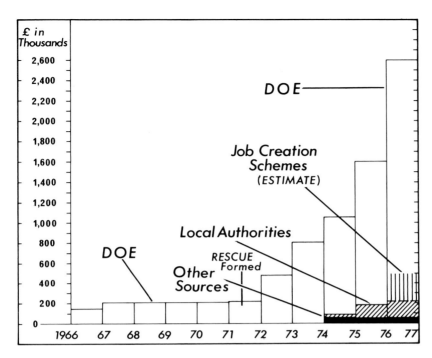

Fig. 47 Diagram showing the sources and scale of finance in rescue archaeology from 1966 to 1977

entered an age of confusion, an administrative shambles of good intentions in which many desired to co-operate but in which the structural framework was unsound. It converted many archaeologists into professional, itinerant committee men, dedicated more to pegging British Rail's annual deficit than to meaningful archaeological activity. Planning integration and priorities, legislation, training, publication and conservation were complex issues for which there was no simple radical solution. Behind the lack of progress made on the promised legislative programme, without which British archaeology could not hope to advance to a more secure position, lurked the government's own Walsh Report only one of whose recommendations, the creation of Acknowledgement Payments to farmers, was put into operation (see p. 44 ff). Yet even that hopeful move to dissuade farmers from damaging scheduled monuments on their land foundered; the disbursement of a mere £620 across two years from 1969 to 1971 in a classic archaeological landscape such as Dorset showed that farmers were simply ignoring the arrangements. Another threat in the countryside, the use of metal detectors to pillage archaeological sites, even those that were theoretically protected, had increased. The unearthing in 1975 of a complete Roman communion service from the scheduled area of the Roman town of Water Newton served to polarise debate on the ethics of treasure hunting, an issue that has continued to dog relations between professional archaeologists, treasure hunters and the British Museum.

Against these debits there remained an all important credit: the annual budget for state-financed archaeology was increasing phenomenally (see Fig.. 47). Increased finance was the first step in any programme born of the 1970s but it spawned a whole series of related problems—questions of organisational structure, legislation, efficiency and cost effectiveness. Logically, of course, the increased finance available should have been accompanied by radical rethinking and restructuring of the methods by which that finance was distributed. In 1973–4 it nearly was. The Department of the Environment expressed itself in favour of the establishment of regional archaeological units that would have approached the long-term ideal of many archaeologists— that is, a decentralised archaeological service. The scheme, however, envisaged substantial support from local authorities, and it was this that led ultimately to the scheme's collapse: county authorities, in particular, were not unnaturally jealous of the right to spend money on a county rather than a regional basis. The failure of the Department of the Environment to create an acceptable national policy resulted in a proliferation of rescue units, committees and trusts as an *ad hoc* solution, and by and large those agencies that were established early on have taken the lion's share of the increased funding available, while latecomers such as Canterbury are under-funded.

Such was the situation that the Rescue Trust and the Council for British Archaeology attempted to fill by presenting in 1974 a joint policy document entitled *Archaeology and Government*. The policy outlined a tiered committee structure that would handle archaeological problems from national to district level in such a way that there would be a firm degree of academic control within the selection of rescue operations. The document was rejected by the Inspectorate, probably because it had been prepared outside Fortress House, and it was received unenthusiastically by many archaeologists. In contrast its reception by local government was warm: many counties welcomed the proposed structure as the first opportunity for archaeologists to state concisely and coherently what they wanted in terms of organisation. By early 1975 the document had become confused by other problems of centralised administration, and by fears that the amateur was being excluded from the running of British archaeology so that the future would lie entirely with the paid professional.

Ultimately, the need for more integrated organisation was recognised in 1974 when the Inspectorate adopted part of the proposals of *Archaeology and Government* by creating as an annexe to the Ancient Monuments Board a National Advisory Committee concerned with

rescue archaeology, together with a series of regional advisory committees designed to examine the academic priorities of rescue archaeology
within their areas. These committees (abolished in 1979), functioned for
several years, and their efficiency varied greatly according to the
character of the various members. The fact that the advisory committees
were limited in the amount of information at their disposal regarding
the effect of redevelopment on archaeology posed a problem; clearly
some areas were poorly served in this respect. Originally local authority
representatives were to be excluded, but the folly of this situation was
quickly reversed. Nor were the committees supposed to discuss finance,
but the division of available funds, largely amongst the actual members
of the committee itself, inevitably formed the main focus of discussion.
The division of the various budgets, however, by the advisory committees ignored the central question of how national finance was to be
divided in regional terms, and such fundamental issues have still not
emerged for public debate.

In the late 1960s and mid-1970s the concept of rescue archaeology as
a simple and straightforward operation faded and the urgent need to
record the evidence of hundreds of sites as they were destroyed became
obvious. By the 1980s that epoch, too, passed, and the picture of the
archaeologist, whether professional or amateur, as a 'helmeted hero
working into the night surrounded by mud, fumes and angry contractors' became the unacceptable face of archaeology. The experiences,
successful and otherwise, of the 1970s brought an improved, more
mature approach. The considered selection of priority tasks and the
employment of greater management skills in marshalling and exploiting
resources made a significant impact on the achievement of proper local,
at times even regional, co-ordination: implicitly or explicitly archaeologists have realised that they no longer operate in isolation, and that
their success depends on establishing working relationships with the
previously alien world of planners and developers. This has proved a
permanent move for the better.

If archaeology's claims for recognition in the planning process are to
be treated seriously, this can only be achieved by justifying them to the
community at large: archaeologists must adequately communicate their
aims, methods and results to the general public, and to those in positions
of authority or influence. Ultimately the support of the wider public is in
itself vital in shaping the opinions of the latter, whether elected
representatives or local authority officers. In the context of economic
stringency archaeology must be seen to be spending money wisely and
capitalising on its relatively limited resources.

Most urban excavation is governed by the constraints of redevelopment that is not archaeologically orientated. The archaeologist is thus at
the mercy of events over which he has no control. On the other hand if

the developer can be sure that efficient excavation is going to take place before he actually develops a site, he is then in a better position to plan his development and will, accordingly, have a more benevolent view of rescue archaeology. During the 1970s great pressures were placed upon developers to become more sensitive to environmental and conservational issues in several fields. Archaeology benefited, and it was not unusual for a financial commitment to be made by the actual developer.

Progress can best be made by recognising from the outset the changed circumstances surrounding excavation today. There have been changes at the archaeological level, with the advent of major urban rescue work, and also at public and local government levels where archaeology increasingly appears as one of many potential environmental or planning constraints. With few exceptions, excavations can no longer be regarded as isolated academic forays conducted by distinguished academics, and there are good indications that many of the new breed of archaeologist are fully aware of this fact. An urban excavation is an intervention in the life of the community, with potential economic, social and educational effects. While this was once strong meat for many archaeologists to accept, contemporary archaeology is so wholly bound up with current environmental and conservational interests that archaeological pressures are now firmly represented in the political arena. In practice, since achievements in regional rescue archaeology stem as often as not from the influence or tenacity of one strong personality, in certain areas the absence of such a figure has meant that relatively little has been achieved.

As the 1970s drew to a close, the financing of British archaeology became the central issue—how it was supplied, where it was spent, and, above all, how it was spent. It had never previously been possible to give more than the most generalised answers to these questions; there had been no overall accounting for the budget of British archaeology, its regional weightings, its biases in favour of particular periods or archaeological fashions, or, most important, its cost effectiveness. What controlled the basic division of finance between regions? Why should the total rescue budget for Scotland in 1974–5 have been only fractionally greater than that for one project in Wales in 1973–4? As a matter of urgency it was necessary to know more about such discrepancies and to find out just what the pound in British archaeology was providing. Was it carpeted offices and a second landrover, or excavations brought to final publication?

In 1976 Rescue embarked on a pioneer survey (*Rescue News* 13, 1977). It represented the first elementary but necessary step towards a fully documented assessment of these questions. However, although it broke valuable new ground, it was ultimately a disappointment: many of its figures were estimates since it is difficult to give exact figures site by site for the budget of rescue archaeology in this country. This is due partly to the mechanics of the Department of the Environment grant system, and partly to the admirable practice of many local authorities of lending tools and equipment, sometimes even staff, to assist excavations within their area. Hidden subsidies of this kind probably contribute another quarter of a million pounds to the real income of British archaeology.

By the late 1970s excavations, with the exception of Coppergate, were being substantially cut back. This is perhaps partly due to 'over success': the great increase in rescue funding during the previous years had led some archaeologists to feel that they had the right to expect full-scale funding from central or local government sources. There was less seeking for assistance outside these channels, but, more recently, the British Gas Corporation and a Water Board have financed excavation. Other nationalised industries and their like, despite their enormous development potential over the last few years, have yet to contribute to the examination of any site threatened by their plans.

Inevitably one awaits the backlash against archaeology. It has enjoyed such favourable publicity over the last few years, such public interest at all levels, that the time must come when its achievements, and above all its costings, will be actively and hostilely questioned. Herein lies the great danger of the more expensive units. With their professional basis and skilled staff they represent the large spenders of British archaeology, spenders whose proximity to the limelight also renders them par-ticularly susceptible to outside criticism. In this respect, therefore, many units would be well advised to devote more time to improving their public image within their community, in justifying and explaining the role of the archaeologist rather than assuming continued existence on a basis of central government funding.

The presence of the large units presents problems. Even as the major fund receivers of British archaeology, it could be fairly said that they receive less than they received in the early 1970s. And the phasing out of an expensive archaeological unit (with all its inevitable vested financial interest) as its goals are achieved remains one of the most difficult tasks for the future. There is some truth in the comment that 'the good in British archaeology is getting better, and the bad worse', and if the development of expensive archaeological units is allowed unchecked, it would make the deprived areas of British archaeology deteriorate still further. In zones where little excavation has been carried out it is notoriously difficult to establish standards and initiatives, and the financing of a team consisting of external volunteers can in effect be counter-productive since it discourages local participation and curtails local voluntary labour.

In this context, therefore, the development of community archaeology on relatively low budgets is something that calls for high priority. It would involve the careful development of work by archaeologists who are prepared to take the necessary time to nurture local involvement and expertise. This is vital if many of the traditional antiquarian societies are to survive in any practical executive form. The question is one of training. Archaeologists tend to be trained in small numbers at universities or merely given advice when volunteering on a dig. The time may well come when grant-giving bodies must insist on an adequate on-going training programme for both staff and volunteers as a condition of granting funds.

There are, however, signs of hope. Hope that stems not so much from the professional debate as from the changing views of the general public. It may be that the creation of a more informed awareness amongst the public will emerge as the most important single archaeological achievement of the 1970s. Although for some people archaeology is still represented by Tutankhamun's tomb, the Acropolis or the Pantheon, there is now a far greater realisation of the significance of Britain's archaeological heritage and the need to study and preserve it. This attitude is far advanced from the crude characterisation of rescue archaeology by a Department of Environment circular in 1975 as the speedy investigation of the evidence contained on sites that are shortly to be destroyed!

Rescue archaeology has been elevated to 'cultural resource management'. In other countries, notably the United States, the federal agencies have to play a more positive role in the maintenance of the historic and cultural environment. There the legislative basis is the National Historic Preservation Act (1966) which established a national register of archaeological sites roughly equivalent to the scheduled monuments and listed buildings in Britain. Yet the American law goes far further by implication in requiring the developer to submit an 'environmental impact statement', an assessment of the effect of the new development on the neighbourhood. It is also the statutory duty of the federal agencies to identify and record archaeological resources in their charge and to ensure that at least one per cent of the development costs of the project are spent on the rescue archaeology necessary.

American thinking is based on a belief that 'the preservation of as much as possible of the resource base . . . for future generations' is a desirable end, beyond the simple mechanics of salvage excavations in the face of destruction. If the achievement of rescue archaeology in Britain in the 1970s is not to be wasted, we must similarly develop an ethic that views our archaeological remains as a non-renewable resource; something to be conserved, if possible, or recorded fully before destruction. The retention of the archaeological site in its context is the best kind of archaeological archive available to the community for the future, fulfilling the objective of archaeology as

> . . . the recreation of the past for the benefit of present and future generations. It is a scientific activity in which, under professional standards of guidance and control the ordinary person, the mature student and on occasion the school child, can take a useful and constructive and educative role . . .

As an element in environmental comprehension, as an educational activity of increasing relevance and potential, archaeology has a considerable role to play in modern society.

To begin to approach this goal, to rationalise all the efforts that were made to improve rescue archaeology in the late 1970s, it was clear that there had to be legislative change, change that would formalise the growing consensus of opinion encouraged by the impact of the archaeologists themselves on the public during that decade. Early in 1979, after years of effort, two archaeological bills came before Parliament. One attempted to rationalise the law concerning treasure trove and the problems surrounding the discovery of valuable objects. It was designed to combat the practice of treasure hunting with metal detectors and to introduce penalties for the concealment of archaeological discoveries. The treasure hunting lobby was also restricted by the second, government-sponsored bill, which went far further than the first.

This was in effect a long-awaited consolidation of existing archaeological legislation. It aimed at the creation of a situation in the planning process whereby urban rescue archaeology would be placed on a firm, guaranteed footing for the first time. Every area in the country would rapidly have some form of officially recognised archaeological personnel, and the penalties for damaging protected monuments whether through the use of metal detectors or otherwise, would be greatly increased.

In April 1979 the bill was passed, but this was not to be the successful culmination of a decade of rapid change and improvement that had characterised rescue archaeology in Britain. The weeks before the bill became an Act the hard-won financial gains of the preceding years were threatened. Central government funding was partly frozen, the academic advisory committees were abolished in the attack on 'quangos' and the Manpower Services Commission's role was drastically curtailed. Of course, these developments were in line with those affecting the country as a whole. Above all, the swift rise in inflation meant that in real terms archaeology was receiving no more, even slightly less, than in the early 1970s: with inadequate allowance for the effects of inflation, the archaeological units across the country were being allocated diminishing funds.

On the face of it there was only one real solution, redundancies, and even closures. The principal cuts appear to have occurred in the South. In one sense at any rate this was sensible: to have cut the budgets of such nascent archaeological organisations in the North as those at Lancaster and Newcastle would have dealt them death-blows. On the other hand, these and other small units cannot be effective when the rise in overheads is so great that there is little left for actual work programmes. The cutbacks meant that the management committee of one such unit had only £6,000 to promote actual work in the field, whether excavation or survey, after the staff salaries and other overheads had been met.

The archaeological organisations that are likely not only to survive but to survive and function effectively are those that have won over local opinion at both public and local authority levels—units that are not wholly dependent on the vagaries of central government funding, especially in the one or two places where the Manpower Services Commission still operates its schemes. True, local authority funding is under as much pressure as that of central government, but, when available, it can respond quicker to the needs created by the unpredictable programmes of redevelopment that characterise periods of recession.

Like so many other aspects of life in the dramatic economic downturn in Britain at the end of the 1970s, archaeology appears as a victim. Yet this in itself reflects an important factor: the rescue revolution moved archaeology as a profession firmly into the public realm of planning and environment. While future generations may be left to assess the academic significance of the results of this revolution the media has taught millions of people that archaeology is not simply concerned with recovering valuable objects from the ground, but with understanding the way in which peoples of the past lived, and even with recreating their history. Archaeology has become far more historically orientated.

The rescue revolution that spanned the 1970s was the greatest single change that has ever taken place in British archaeology. It has set the shape and organisation of archaeology in this country. Like all such substantive advances in the academic sphere it was effected in the face of bureaucratic opposition and professional hostilities. That it happened at all was due to the harnessing of public opinion. But its results have been far short of those of a full state archaeology service that could have solved the problems of the existing situation. The pattern is now set for the foreseeable future, until, perhaps, a second rescue revolution completes the task.

Postscript

Since the Ancient Monuments and Archaeological Areas Bill passed to the Statute Book, the effects of its implementation have been awaited with increasing suspicion by archaeologists. How many zones would be described as areas of archaeological importance across the country as a whole? Archaeologists probably envisaged a total reaching three figures, but the Department of the Environment Inspectorate proposed establishing areas of archaeological importance at only 10 historic centres: Berwick-on-Tweed, Canterbury, Chester, Colchester, Exeter, Gloucester, Hereford, Lincoln, Oxford and York. While progress will probably be forthcoming at most of these cities, the prospects are not entirely convincing. The planning departments of Lincoln and Gloucester, classic examples of historic cities with predictable archaeological cores, have each apparently succeeded in refusing to accept designation as a zone of an area of archaeological importance. The designation was intended, not to stop redevelopment, but to guarantee time for archaeological investigation to take place between redevelopment replanning and actual reconstruction. The auguries are not good, and it is difficult not to relate the *de facto* non-implementation of the Act to prevailing governmental attitudes.

This is very clearly the case in Mr Heseltine's proposals for the disestablishment of the Inspectorate of Ancient Monuments as a branch of the Department of the Environment and its resurrection in the form of a 'quango' orientated towards a more commercial running of the ancient monuments and historic buildings currently in the charge of the Department. The very radical proposals will probably be implemented (by April 1984), unless they meet insuperable opposition; and such opposition is unlikely to come from the archaeological forum. Many archaeologists have become considerably disillusioned with the current working methods of those branches of the Department of the Environment responsible for ancient monuments, and a cautious welcome has been given to the proposals, provided they are qualified in a detailed and responsible way as promised, particularly in respect of rescue archaeology which is barely mentioned at all.

At present the Department of the Environment has many and varied functions: the scheduling of Ancient Monuments; the care and maintenance of those buildings and monuments that are under the charge of the government; the listing of buildings of historic or architectural interest; and the funding of rescue excavations. If the proposed changes are realised, then central government's functions would be reduced considerably and the administration of listed buildings and ancient monuments would also be altered. Mr Heseltine's new body would be responsible for the care and maintenance of buildings under national ownership, for grants for listed buildings and for work in conservation areas. It would also promote sales of literature and advertising, would advise the rump section of the Department on the listing of buildings and the custodianship of national monuments, and co-ordinate rescue archaeology. While eliminating responsibility for some matters, others would remain under the control of the Secretary of State.

Most people would not object in principle to the idea of a 'quango' in control of Ancient Monuments and Historic Buildings, but there is the possibility in all this that the government is seen to be doing nothing less than creating a 'quango' in order to reduce civil servants and follow current political dogma. Archaeologists see the historic past of this country as the responsibility of the government, a responsibility that it has taken decades to achieve and one that should not be subject in any way to political manoeuvring. It is clear that the success of the proposed new changes would depend on the quality of the mangement team and its Chief Executive. Archaeologists feel that our national heritage cannot be equated with a profit and loss account; funding for the proposed change may at worst be at the level for corresponding branches of the Department of the Environment, and the royal palaces, for example, are omitted from the proposals, thus excluding the Tower of London and Hampton Court, two of the three principal money-spinners in Britain's tourist heritage.

Non-archaeological interests, especially those of the County Councils Association on whose members new and possibly unwelcome respons-ibility must fall, have an important part to play in the debate preceding the government's proposed revolution in the structure of British archaeology. The first revolution that began 12 years ago was very different—a spontaneous pressure for improvement that saw academics learn that they had to adopt very non-academic methods to promote change from government quarters. That first revolution was a success: it vastly expanded practical archaeology in Britain and created a new generation of official archaeologists. This new generation has now to relearn the methods of influencing government policy, if the hard-won overall growth and improvement in archaeology is to continue to the end of the millennium.

Appendix:
Getting in touch with your local archaeologist

This book has told the story of many new archaeological organisations that have been created. If you want to report a find to your local archaeologist, or get in touch with a view to volunteering your assistance for the future, you will find the following list of use. Section I lists the names and addresses of the County Archaeologists now established in most of Britain's local authorities. Sometimes the County Archaeologists are also the directors of a field team in their area, in which case their names re-appear in Section II where active archaeological units are listed along with the name of the director, the address and telephone number.

I. County Archaeological Officers

Bedfordshire
D. BAKER
Principal Conservation Officer
Planning Department
County Hall
Caudwell Street
BEDFORD
0234–63222 Ext 64

Berkshire
P. CHADWICK
Shire Hall
Shinfield Park
READING

Buckinghamshire
M. FARLEY
Buckinghamshire County Museum
Church Street
AYLESBURY HP20 2QP
0296–82158/88849

Cambridgeshire
Ms. A. TAYLOR
County Planning Department
Shire Hall
CAMBRIDGE
0223–58977

Cheshire
S. R. WILLIAMS
Principal Archaeologist
County Planning Department
Commerce House
CHESTER CH1 1SN
0244–603163

Cleveland
Miss M. BROWN
County Archaeologist
County of Cleveland
Halifax Buildings
Exchange Place
MIDDLESBROUGH
0642–40668

Clwyd
J. MANLEY
Clwyd Archaeology Officer
Planning Department
County Hall
MOLD Clwyd
0352–2121

Coventry
Miss M. RYLATT
Field Officer
32 Middlesborough Road
COVENTRY
0203–25555

Cumbria
T. CLARE
Archaeological Officer
County Planning Office
KENDAL
0539–21000

Devon
P. CHILD
County Planning Department
County Hall
EXETER EX2 4QL
0392–77977 Ext 325

Dorset
L. KEEN
County Archaeologist
Planning Department
County Hall
DORCHESTER DT1 1XJ
0505–3131 Ext 4280

Durham
P. CLACK
Co. Durham Archaeology Officer
c/o Department of Archaeology
12 Saddler Street
DURHAM
0385–64466

Essex
J. HEDGES
County Archaeologist
Planning Department
County Hall
CHELMSFORD CH1 1LF
0245–67222 Ext 2388

Grampian
I. SHEPHERD
Grampian Regional Council
Department of Physical Planning
Woodhill House
Ashgrove West
ABERDEEN AB9 2LW
0224–68222 Ext 2412

Hampshire
M. HUGHES
County Archaeologist
County Planning Department
Hampshire County Council
The Castle
WINCHESTER
0962–4411 Ext 7243

Hereford and Worcester
C. ROBERTS
County Museum
Hartlebury Castle
KIDDERMINSTER DY11 7XZ
029–96–416

Hertfordshire
T. M. JEFFREY
County Planning Department
County Hall
HERTFORD SG13 8DN
0992–45242 Ext 5189

Lancashire
B. J. N. EDWARDS
Lancashire Record Office
Bow Lane
PRESTON PR1 2RE
0772–51905

Lincolnshire
P. EVERSON
c/o County Planning Department
Newland
LINCOLN
0522–29931

Merseyside
County Museums Department
William Brown Street
LIVERPOOL L3 8EN
051–2075451 Ext 14

Northamptonshire
A. HANNAN
County Architects Department
Wootton Hall Park
NORTHAMPTON NN4 9BQ
0604–63131 Ext 271

North Yorkshire
M. GRIFFITHS
County Planning Department
County Hall
NORTHALLERTON
0609–3123 Ext 533

Nottinghamshire
M. BISHOP
Department of Planning &
  Transportation
County Hall
West Bridgeford,
NOTTINGHAM
0602–866555

Shropshire
Planning Department
Salop County Council
Shire Hall
Abbey Foregate
SHREWSBURY
0743–222332

Somerset
I. BURROW
Archaeological Officer
County Planning Department
County Hall
TAUNTON
0823–3451 Ext 232

South Yorkshire
J. H. LITTLE
County Archaeologist
Cultural Activities Centre
Ellin Street
SHEFFIELD S1 4PL
0742–29191 Ext 31

Staffordshire
K. SHERIDAN
County Planning Department
Martin Street
STAFFORD ST16 2LE
0785–3121 Ext 7282

Stirling
Mrs L. MAIN
Planning Department
Central Regional Council
Viewforth
STIRLING
Central Scotland FK8 2ET
0786–3111 Ext 201

Suffolk
S. WEST
County Archaeologist
Planning Department
Shire Hall
BURY ST EDMUNDS
0284–63141 Ext 450

Surrey
D. G. BIRD
County Archaeological Officer
County Planning Department
KINGSTON-ON-THAMES
01–546–1050 Ext 3665

Tayside
Miss L. THOMS
Tayside Archaeological Officer
City Museum & Art Gallery
Albert Square
DUNDEE
0382–645443

Tyne and Wear
Miss R. B. HARBOTTLE
Museum and Art Gallery
8 Higham Place
NEWCASTLE-UPON-TYNE
  NE1 8AG
0632–816144 Ext 259

Warwickshire
Ms H. MACLAGAN
Field Archaeologist
County Museum
Market Place
WARWICK
0926–43431

West Sussex
F. G. ALDSWORTH
Archaeological Officer
County Planning Department
County Hall
Tower Street
CHICHESTER
0243–85100 Ext 682

West Yorkshire
County Archaeologist
Department of Recreation and Arts
County Hall
WAKEFIELD WF1 2QW
0924–67111

Wiltshire
W. FORD
Archaeological Officer
Library and Museums
20 Sythesea Road
TROWBRIDGE
022–14–3641 Ext 36

II. Units/Committees

Bedfordshire County Archaeological Unit
D. Baker
Bedfordshire County Council
County Hall
BEDFORD MK42 9AP
0234–63222 Ext 64

Bristol City Museum Unit
M. Ponsford
Bristol City Museum
Queen's Road
BRISTOL 8
0272–27256

Canterbury Archaeological Trust
T. W. T. Tatton-Brown
92A Broad Street
CANTERBURY
Kent CT1 2QU
0227–62062

Carlisle Archaeological Unit
M. McCarthy
Planning Department
Civic Centre
CARLISLE
0228–23411

Chelmsford Excavation Committee
P. J. Drury
31 Nursery Road
CHELMSFORD
Essex

Chichester Excavations Unit
A. Down
8 North Palant
CHICHESTER
Sussex
0245–785166 Ext 122

Clwyd–Powys Archaeological Trust
C. R. Musson
7a Church Street
WELSHPORT
Powys SY21 7DL
0938–3670

Colchester Archaeological Unit
P. Crummy
East Hill House
76 High Street
COLCHESTER
Essex 0206–41051

Cornwall Committee for Rescue Archaeology
Sites and Monuments Record Unit
3 Strangeways Terrace
TRURO

CRAAGS (Committee for Rescue
    Archaeology in Avon, Gloucester and
    Somerset)
T. Courtney
The Archaeological Centre
Mark Lane
BRISTOL

Devon Archaeological Committee
c/o Mrs H. Miles, Hon Secretary
Dept of Extra-Mural Studies
University of Exeter
EXETER EX4 3QN

Doncaster Metropolitan Borough Council
P. Buckland
Museums and Arts Service
Chequer Road
DONCASTER
South Yorks
0302–62095/60814

Dyfed Archaeological Trust
D. Benson
The Bishop's Palace
Abergwili
CARMARTHEN
0267–31667

Essex County Council
Planning Department
County Hall
CHELMSFORD CM1 1LF
0245–67222 Ext 2388

Glamorgan–Gwent Archaeological Trust
G. Dowdell
6 Prospect Place
Swansea
GLAMORGAN
0792–55208

Gloucester City Excavation Unit
Ms. C. Heighway
Barbican Road
GLOUCESTER GL1 2JF
0452–26342

Greater Manchester Archaeological Unit
P. Mayes
Department of Archaeology
Manchester University
MANCHESTER M13 9PL
061–273–3333 Ext 3472

Grosvenor Museum Excavations Section,
    Chester
T. J. Strickland
27 Grosvenor Street
CHESTER
0244–21616

Gwynedd Archaeological Trust
R. D. White
Deiniel Road
Bangor
GWYNEDD
0248–52535

Humberside Archaeological Committee
B. Whitwell
c/o Hull Museum
23 High Street
HULL
0482–28115

Kingston-upon-Thames Museum
M. Smith
Fairfield West
KINGSTON-UPON-THAMES
Surrey
01–546–8905

Leicestershire County Council Archaeological
Field Unit
Ms J. E. Mellor
Leicestershire Museums
96 New Walk
LEICESTER LE1 6TD
0533–554100

Lincoln Archaeological Trust
M. J. Jones
The Sessions House
Lindum Road
LINCOLN LN2 1PB
0522–217511

London & Middlesex Archaeological Society
(LAMAS) Inner London North Unit
Ms I. Schwab
D. Whip
Imox House
42 Theobalds Road
LONDON WC1

Milton Keynes Development Corporation
D. Mynard
Bradwell Abbey Field Centre
Bradwell
MILTON KEYNES MK13 9AP
0908–312475

Museum of London
Department of Urban Archaeology
B. Hobley
71 Basinghall Street
LONDON EC2
01–606–1933/4/5

Nene Valley Research Committee
Mr D. F. Mackreth
Archaeological Field Centre
Ham Lane
Orton Waterville
PETERBOROUGH PE2 0UU
0733–233757

Norfolk Archaeological Unit
P. Wade-Martins
Union House
GRESSENHALL
Norfolk NR20 4DR
036–286–528/9

North-East England Archaeological Unit
C. O'Brien
Department of Archaeology
The University
NEWCASTLE-UPON-TYNE
  NE1 7RU
0632–328511 Ext 4130

North Yorkshire County Council
M. Griffiths
County Planning Department
County Hall
NORTHALLERTON DL7 8AQ
0609–3123 Ext 533

Norwich Survey
A. Carter
c/o Centre for East Anglian Studies
University of East Anglia
NORWICH NR4 7TJ
Norfolk
0603–22233

Northampton Development Corporation
J. Williams
Cliftonville House
Bedford Road
NORTHAMPTON
0604–46444

Oxfordshire Archaeological Unit
T. G. Hassall
46 Hythe Bridge Street
OXFORD OX1 2EP
0865–43888

Passmore Edwards Museum
P. Wilkinson
Romford Road
  Stratford
LONDON E15 4LZ
01–534–4545 Ext 376

Poole Museums Archaeological Unit
Guildhall Museum
Market Street
POOLE
Dorset
020–13–2925

South Yorkshire County Council
J. H. Little
Dept of Recreation
Culture & Health
Ellin Street
SHEFFIELD
0742–29191

Southampton Archaeological Research
    Committee
M. Brisbane
25A Oxford Street
SOUTHAMPTON
0703–32631

Southwark and Lambeth Archaeological
    Excavation Committee
H. Sheldon
Old Port Medical Centre
English Grounds
Morgans Lane
LONDON SE1
01–407–1989

S W London Unit
S. Macracken
Castle Arch
GUILDFORD
Surrey GU1 3SX
0483–70150

Sussex Archaeological Field Unit
P. L. Drewett
c/o Institute of Archaeology
31–34 Gordon Square
LONDON WC1H 0PY
01–387–6052

Trent Valley Archaeological Research
    Committee
c/o The University
NOTTINGHAM NG7 2RD
0602–56101

Verulamium Museum and Excavation Unit
G. D. Davies
St Michael's
ST ALBANS
Herts
0727–54659/59919

Wessex Archaeological Unit
Rougemont
Rougemont Close
SALISBURY
Wilts
0722–28091

West Yorkshire County Council
J. Hedges
County Hall
WAKEFIELD
West Yorks WF1 2QW
0924–67111

City of Winchester Rescue Archaeology Unit
K. Qualmann
City Archaeologist
Winchester City Museums
75 Hyde Street
WINCHESTER
Hants
0962–68166

York Archaeological Trust
P. V. Addyman
47 Aldwalk
YORK YO1 2BX
0904–59777

Bibliography

General

M. Biddle, D. Hudson and C. Heighway, *The Future of London's Past*, Rescue, 1973.

R. Allen Brown, H. M. Colvin and A. J. Taylor, *The History of the King's Works* I, HMSO, 1963.

R. Beresford Dew, 'Rescue Archaeology: Finance 1976–77', *Rescue News* 13, Spring 1977, 4–6.

R. G. Collingwood, *An Autobiography*, Oxford, 1939.

O. G. S. Crawford, 'Editorial Notes', *Antiquity* III, 9, 1929.

Lord Esher, *York, a Study in Conservation*, HMSO, 1968.

W. F. Grimes, *Excavations in Roman and Medieval London*, 1968.

Mortimer Wheeler, 'Caistor, and a Comment', *Antiquity* III, 10, 1929.

Rescue 'Rescue Financial Survey', *Rescue News* 10, Winter 1975, 12.

Chapter 2

P. A. Barker, *Excavations on the Site of the baths basilica at Wroxeter, 1966–71: an interim report*, University of Birmingham, 1971; and *1966–74: an interim report*, *Britannia VI*, 1975, 106–17.

Ministry of Transport *Buchanan Report: Traffic in Towns*, HMSO, 1963.

CBA, *The Buchanan Report and Historic Towns*, 1964.

B. W. Cunliffe, *The past tomorrow*, an inaugural lecture, Southampton University (8th December 1969), 1970.

P. J. Fowler, *Approaches to Archaeology*, London, 1977.

P. J. Fowler and D. Miles, *Tewkesbury: the archaeological implications of development*, Tewkesbury Archaeological & Architectural Committee/Rescue, 1973.

'For New Archaeology', *The Listener*, 20th January–2nd March 1972.

C. M. Heighway (ed), CBA, *The Erosion of History: archaeology and planning in towns*, 1972.

CBA, *Historic Towns*, 1965.

M. G. Jarrett, 'A revolution in British Archaeology?' *Antiquity* XLVII, 1973, 193–6.

R. Milne, Archaeology: a planning battlefield, *Surveyor*, 12 July 1974.

P. Rahtz, 'Rescue' and Archaeology in the West Midlands, *Midland History*, 1972, 1–10.

P. Rahtz (ed), *Rescue Archaeology*, Penguin, 1974.

C. Thomas, 'Ethics in Archaeology', *Antiquity*, XLV 1971, 268–74.

Chapter 3

D. Benson and D. Miles, *The upper Thames valley: an archaeological survey of the river gravels*, Oxford, 1974. (Illustrates how air photography constantly increases the number of known sites, many of which merit scheduling.)

A. M. Jackson, *Forestry and archaeology*, Rescue, 1978.

G. D. B. Jones, 'Crisis in Archaeology', *Journal of Environmental Planning*, 1973, 1 ff.

Sir David Walsh (Chairman), *Walsh Report*: Report of the Committee of Enquiry into the arrangements for the protection of field monuments, 1966–8, HMSO, 1969 (reprinted 1972).

Chapter 5

P. J. Fowler (ed), 'M5, M4 and Archaeology', CBA Groups XII, XIII: *Archaeological Review* 4, 1969, 13–20.
Durobrivae: A useful annual summary of work in the Nene Valley.

P. J. Fowler, 'Field archaeology on the M5 motorway 1969–71', *Field Survey in British Archaeology* (ed E. Fowler), CBA, 1972, 28–38.

F. M. M. Pryor, 'A Possible House of the Neolithic Period at Fengate', *Durobrivae* I, 1973, 18.

F. M. M. Pryor, *Prehistoric Man in the Nene Valley*, Nene Valley Research Committee Publications, 1973.

C. C. Taylor, *Peterborough New Town: A Survey of the Antiquities in the Areas of Development*, Royal Commission for Ancient Monuments, 1969.

J. P. Wild, 'Longthorpe, an essay in continuity', *Durobrivae* I, 1973, 7 ff.

J. P. Wild, *The Romans in the Nene Valley*, Nene Valley Research Committee Publications, 1972.

J. H. Williams, 'Two Iron Age Sites in Northampton', *Northampton Development Corporation, Archaeological Monograph No 1*, 1974.

Chapter 6

J. Collis, *Exeter Excavations: The Guildhall Site*, 1972.

C. Colyer, 'Excavations at Lincoln 1970–2', *Antiquaries Journal* LV, 1975, 227 ff.

C. Colyer, *Lincoln: the archaeology of an historic city*, Lincoln Archaeological Trust, 1975.

P. Crummy, *Colchester: recent excavations and research*, Colchester Excavation Committee, 1974.

P. Crummy, 'Excavations at Colchester', *Britannia* VII.

H. Hurst, 'Excavations at Gloucester 1971–3': second interim report, *Antiquaries Journal* LIV, 1974, Pt I, 8 ff. Third interim report, *Antiquaries Journal* LV, 1975, 267 ff.

Chapter 7

G. D. B. Jones, *Excavations at Moridunum, Carmarthen*, Carmarthenshire Antiquary, 1969, 70.

W. H. Manning, *The Roman Legionary Fortress at Usk*.

The Welsh Trusts publish annual reports of their work; that of the Glamorgan–Gwent Trust is particularly informative.

Chapter 8

G. G. Simpson (ed), *Scotland's Medieval Burghs: an archaeological heritage in danger*, Edinburgh, 1972.
(This booklet sets out, for the first time, the archaeological potential of Scotland's historic towns. Its influence was therefore considerable in stirring up informed interest, although some of the assessments can now be seen to underestimate the potential recovery of information from excavation.)

I. Crawford, 'The destruction in the Highlands and Islands of Scotland', in *Rescue Archaeology* (ed. P. A. Rahtz), Penguin, 1974.
(A trenchant and largely unanswerable attack on the inertia and ineffectiveness of Scotland's official archaeological service at the time.)

M. E. C. Stewart and L. M. Thoms, *It will soon be too late*, Perth, 1976.
(An archaeological survey of Perth prior to the High Street excavations.)

N. Q. Bogdan and J. W. Wordsworth, *The medieval excavations at the High Street, Perth*, 1975–6: an interim report, 1978.

Chapter 9

P. V. Addyman, *2000 Years of York—the Archaeological Story*, 1979.

P. V. Addyman, *Rescue Archaeology in York*, Elgee Memorial Lecture, 1973.

P. V. Addyman and J. H. Rumsby, *The Archaeological Implications of Proposed Development in York*, Yorks. Phil. Soc./CBA, 1972.

P. V. Addyman *et al.*, Facsimilies of the *Excavations in York* (designed to comprise 18 vols.), published by the CBA, are available on most of the recent excavations.

P. C. Buckland, 'Archaeology and environment in York', *Journal of Archaeological Science*, 1974, I, 303 ff.

B. Hope-Taylor, *Under York Minster*, 1972.
Interim: A quarterly bulletin available to subscribers describing the latest developments at York. Obtainable from the York Archaeological Trust.

R. Merrifield, *The Roman City of London*, London, 1965.

B. Hobley and J. Schofield, 'Excavations in the City of London: first interim report', *Antiquaries Journal* LVII, 1977, 31 ff.

B. Hobley, *Popular Archaeology*, September 1979, 33 ff.

See further *Popular Archaeology*, June, July, September, 1982.

Chapter 10

P. J. Fowler, *Approaches to Archaeology*, London, 1977.

G. D. B. Jones, editorials in *Popular Archaeology*, a monthly magazine for the public. Obtainable direct from *Popular Archaeology*, 24 Barton Street, Bath, Avon. 0225–64794.

Current Archaeology, a quarterly magazine. Obtainable from 9 Nassington Road, London NW3 2TX.

M. G. Jarrett, *Antiquity* XLIX, 1975. (A counterblast to F. H. Thompson, 'Rescue archaeology: research or rubbish collection?')

P. A. Rahtz, 'What kind of Regional Units do we need?', *Rescue News* 4, Summer 1974, 2–5.

M. Biddle, *Archaeology and government: a plan for archaeology in Britain*, Rescue/CBA, 1974.

   Rescue News: Offers an up to date account of current issues in rescue archaeology. Obtainable from Rescue.

F. H. Thompson, 'Rescue archaeology: research or rubbish collection?' *Antiquity* XLIX, 1975, 43–5.

Rescue Archaeology: Papers from the First New World Conference on Rescue Archaeology, eds. R. L. Wilson and G. Loyola (National Trust for Historic Preservation Organisation of American States), 1983.

Index